I0171719

Come Lord Jesus Come

Come Lord Jesus Come

Vinu V Das

TP
Tabor Press

© 2025 Tabor Press. All rights reserved. No part of this publication may be reproduced, distributed, or transmitted in any form or by any means without the prior written permission of the publisher, except in the case of brief quotations embodied in critical reviews and certain other noncommercial uses permitted by copyright law.

ISBN 978-1-997541-20-2

Table of Contents

Chapter 1. Maranatha—The Church's Ancient Cry

From the catacombs of Rome to the desert cells of Egypt, from soaring Gregorian chants to Puritan pulpits, the church has carried a single, undimmed longing: "Maranatha—Come, Lord Jesus." This simple Aramaic cry, uttered in moments of suffering and serenity alike, binds every age of believers in a shared expectation that the King who first came in humility will one day return in glory. Embedded in the last words of Scripture and echoed in the catacomb inscriptions, Maranatha is more than an expression of wishful thinking; it is the church's heartbeat, converging divine promise and human hope into a single, urgent plea.

Christ's own teaching and the apostolic witness cast this expectation in both immediate and cosmic dimensions. While we already taste the reality of the kingdom in Word and sacrament, each echo of "Come, Lord Jesus" reminds us that the fullness of redemption remains just beyond our horizon. In worship, we give voice to this tension of the "already and not yet," celebrating what Christ has accomplished and yearning for what remains to be fulfilled. Through every liturgy, hymn, and prayer the church discovers that calling upon His name is itself an act of faith, an anchor for the soul amid trial and a spark of joy amid waiting.

As we trace the journey of Maranatha—from Aramaic lips to modern devotionals—we will explore how this cry shaped the church's history, informed its theology, and continues to fuel its mission. Our study of Maranatha will not only ground us in biblical truth but also ignite our own longing, reminding us that the church's ancient cry remains the church's living hope.

1.1 Historical Echoes of "Come"

1.1.1 Persecution and Longing in the Catacombs

From the mid-first century through the early fourth, Christians meeting in Rome and elsewhere risked arrest, confiscation of property, even death. Beneath the city streets, in the dimly lit tunnels of the catacombs, believers carved reminders of hope: anchors, fish, and sometimes the Aramaic word "Maranatha" itself. These secret services were a testament to a faith that refused to be silenced, a faith anchored in the promise, "Surely I am with you always" (Matt 28:20). In that subterranean gloom, the cry "Come, Lord Jesus" became both a prayer for deliverance from earthly persecution and a longing for His eternal reign (Rev 22:20). As families huddled together, reading Paul's words about "an inheritance that can never perish... kept in heaven for you" (1 Pet 1:4), their lips whispered Maranatha, affirming both a present comfort and a future hope. The catacomb walls, decorated with simple murals of the Good Shepherd, reminded them that Christ Himself was already with them, guiding them through every trial (John 10:14–15). Thus even in death's shadow, "Maranatha" rang out as the church's heartbeat—anticipating the day when mourning would end and every tear wiped away (Rev 21:4).

1.1.2 Desert Fathers' Yearning in Solitude

By the third century, disciples of Anthony, Pachomius, and other desert mothers and fathers withdrew into the Egyptian sands, seeking an undistracted encounter with God. Their daily rhythm of prayer, fasting, and manual labor was punctuated by the cry of the heart: Maranatha—Come, Lord Jesus—echoing through their solitary cells. Drawing on Psalms such as "As the deer pants for streams of water, so my soul pants for you, my God" (Ps 42:1), they embodied the soul's thirst for the King. In their ceaseless watch, they heard echoes of Paul's charge to "pray without ceasing" (1 Thess 5:17), transforming the austere desert into a sanctuary of unceasing expectation. Their reports of visions—of Christ's radiant form guiding their steps—fueled a wider monastic movement that spread across the Near East. In these lives of radical detachment, Maranatha was not merely a future plea but a present prayer, aligning their hearts with the "already and not yet" reality of Christ's kingdom (Luke 17:21). Through their example, later generations saw that withdrawal from the world could intensify, rather than diminish, the church's longing for the Bridegroom's return.

1.1.3 Medieval Pilgrims and the Hope of Homecoming

As Europe emerged from the fall of Rome, the medieval pilgrim set out—often on foot—for holy sites such as Jerusalem, Compostela, or Canterbury, seeing each step as both atonement and anticipation. Psalms of pilgrimage ("I rejoiced with those who said to me, 'Let us go to the house of the LORD'" – Ps 122:1) were sung in Latin: "Domine, veni!"— Lord, come! In convents and abbeys, the chant "Maranatha" wove through the Divine Office, reminding monks and nuns that their ultimate pilgrimage lay beyond this age. Weathering bandits, illness, and rugged terrain, pilgrims confessed that true homecoming awaited the day when Christ himself would call them across the Jordan of death into everlasting rest (Rev 21:1–2). Their badges—water-worn flints from the Jordan River, scallop shells from Spain—became tangible symbols of a spiritual journey toward the heavenly Jerusalem (Heb 12:22–24). In cathedral sermons on the Last Judgment, bishops urged the faithful to "keep watch" (Matt 24:42), framing every pilgrimage as a rehearsal for the final gathering before the throne. Thus, from cobblestone roads to cathedral crypts, the medieval church lived in the tension of pilgrimage: already citizens of earth, yet ever yearning for the "City whose architect and builder is God" (Heb 11:10).

1.2 New Testament Foundations

1.2.1 Revelation 22:17 – Invitation to the Thirsty

John's closing exhortation in Revelation—"The Spirit and the bride say, 'Come!' " (Rev 22:17)—frames the return of Christ as an open invitation extending to every soul. Here the "Spirit" represents God's active witness through the lives of believers, while the "bride" symbolizes the collective church longing for her Bridegroom. The image of "whosoever will" drinking freely of the water of life echoes Old Testament promises ("Ho, everyone who thirsts, come to the waters" – Isa 55:1), yet now the waters are offered by the One who conquered death (John 4:14). In first-century house churches, this verse would have galvanized persecuted believers, reminding them that God's grace is not rationed but lavishly poured out on all who yearn for Him. The communal voice of "The Spirit and the bride" also underscores the unity of God's work: divine initiative meets human response. Every hymn or prayer drawn from this text becomes more than theology—it is a living plea, imbued with both urgency ("Come quickly!") and open arms for every seeker (Rev 22:20).

1.2.2 Revelation 22:20 – The Promise of Return

Immediately following the invitation, John records Christ's assurance: "He who testifies to these things says, 'Yes, I am coming soon.' Amen. Come, Lord Jesus!" (Rev 22:20). The double "Yes" of the Greek original (Nai, nai) conveys emphatic certainty: this promise is irrevocable. Early Christians would have tattooed these words on their minds when Paul warned that scoffers would deride the doctrine of Christ's return (2 Pet 3:3–4). Yet here stands the unshakable testimony of the risen

Lord Himself—He who holds "the keys of Death and Hades" (Rev 1:18) declares His imminent advent. Liturgically, the Church has echoed this verse in every season, but especially in Advent and at the Lord's Supper, transforming remembrance of Christ's first coming into expectancy for His second. The fragile boundary between "already" and "not yet" trembles with hope: the same Jesus who walked dusty roads will return on clouds of glory (Acts 1:11). And so "Maranatha!" becomes not a sentimental wish but a confident confession— Christ is coming, and all creation awaits His unveiling.

1.2.3 Titus 2:13 – "Blessed Hope" in Pauline Thought

Writing to young pastor Titus, Paul urges him to instruct believers "to live self-controlled, upright, and godly lives in this present age, while we wait for the blessed hope—the appearing of the glory of our great God and Savior, Jesus Christ" (Titus 2:12–13). The phrase "blessed hope" (elpis makaria) captures both the joy and the certainty of what is promised: not a vague wish but a sure inheritance reserved in heaven (1 Pet 1:4). For Paul, this eschatological anticipation is the bedrock of Christian ethics—holiness flows from hope. In congregations scattered by persecution or hardship, teaching on the "appearing" galvanized believers to patient endurance (Rom 8:23–25) and fervent holiness (1 John 3:2–3). It also recasts suffering in light of future glory: trials are momentary when measured against eternity (2 Cor 4:17). Throughout the early church—and even today—Titus 2:13 stands at the intersection of doctrine and devotion: Christ's return is both our anchor in storm and our motivation for godliness. Thus, Maranatha ! is not mere anticipation, but the power that transforms how we live now.

1.3 Theological Meaning of "Maranatha"

1.3.1 Aramaic Nuances: Imperative and Perfect Tense

The word "Maranatha" derives from two Aramaic forms: מ.ר.ן (maran, "our Lord") in the **imperative** ("Come!") and אות.נות.א (athnatha, "has come") in the **perfect** tense. This duality captures both a command and a completed action—Christ's return is both urgently desired and already guaranteed by His first coming. In the early church's Semitic milieu, such a phrase would ring with the force of divine authority: to call "Lord, come!" is to summon One whose victory over death is already accomplished (Col 1:18). It also echoes Jesus' own words, "I am with you always" (Matt 28:20), reassuring believers that His presence transcends time. Thus, every Maranatha-prayer carries within it a confession that Jesus has inaugurated His kingdom and an expectation that He will consummate it. This Aramaic flavor reminds us that Christian hope is rooted in history: the One who once dwelt among us remains our living Lord—even as we yearn for His visible return (Rev 1:7).

1.3.2 Christ's "Already and Not Yet" Presence

"Maranatha" encapsulates the gospel tension of the kingdom: Christ's reign is **already** inaugurated in His death and resurrection, yet **not yet** fully unveiled until His second coming. Paul affirms that we "have been raised with Christ" (Col 3:1), and yet we groan inwardly "until we are adopted" (Rom 8:23). Similarly, Jesus declares, "The kingdom of God is in your midst" (Luke 17:21), even as He warns that "no one knows the day or hour" of its consummation (Matt 25:13). This paradox fuels both our confidence—knowing the decisive victory is won—and our longing—for the day when every enemy is finally put under His feet (1 Cor 15:25). In worship, we already taste "the water of life" (Rev 22:17), yet we echo the bride's refrain, "Come, Lord Jesus!" because the fullness of joy awaits His unveiled presence (1 John 3:2). Embracing this tension sustains the church through trials: we work and witness now, trusting that today's labors bear fruit in tomorrow's glory.

1.3.3 Eschatological Tension: Now-and-Not-Yet Kingdom

The eschatological tension of Maranatha shapes Christian living: we live **now** in the reality of resurrection power, yet we anticipate **not yet** the final restoration of all things. Hebrews reminds us that Abraham "looked forward" to a city built by God (Heb 11:10), while Peter urges believers to live holy lives "since you are waiting for these things" (2 Pet 3:11–12). Our daily discipleship—acts of mercy, pursuit of justice, and proclamation of the gospel—reflects the kingdom that has broken into history (Matt 25:34–40), even as we await its full manifestation. The Reformation's slogan, *Ecclesia reformata, semper reformanda* ("the church reformed, always reforming"), stems from this dynamic: because Christ is coming again, we must continually align our structures, worship, and witness with His royal will. Thus Maranatha is not passive resignation but active expectancy: every prayer, every good work, and every moment of faithful endurance testifies that the age to come is both our heritage and our hope (Rev 21:1–4). In this tension, the church stands as a foretaste of the New Heavens and New Earth while crying out in unison, "Come, Lord Jesus, come!"

1.4 Maranatha in Early Christian Worship

1.4.1 Use in Prayers and Litanies of the East

In the Eastern churches, as early as the late second century, "Maranatha" was woven into the very fabric of communal prayer. The *Didache* (Teaching of the Twelve Apostles) exhorts believers to pray "three times each day" and to invoke the Lord's return as they offer thanksgiving and supplication (Didache 8:2–3). By the fourth century, the Liturgy of St. James included a response after the Sanctus: "Blessed is He who comes in the name of the Lord. Maranatha!" echoing Jesus' triumphal entry (Matt 21:9). In these gatherings, the deacon's call for intercession ("Let us pray for those in affliction...") was followed by the congregation's unified cry, "Maranatha—Come, Lord Jesus," thus blending petition for present needs with eschatological longing (Phil 4:6). The Cappadocian Fathers—Basil, Gregory, and Gregory— affirmed that this liturgical praxis rooted worship in both Scripture and expectation, drawing on Isaiah's oracle, "O that You would rend the heavens and come down" (Isa 64:1). Such usage underscored that each Eucharistic celebration was itself a "taste" of the heavenly banquet yet to be fully revealed (1 Cor 11:26). Through centuries of persecution and doctrinal controversy, Eastern Christians maintained that every doxology should ascend with Maranatha, keeping the hope of Christ's return ever before the church's eyes.

1.4.2 Incorporation into Western Chant and Hymnody

Western Christendom likewise embraced Maranatha in its burgeoning hymn tradition, especially during the Medieval and Reformation periods. The Latin hymn *"Veni, Veni, Emmanuel"*—first sung in monastic cloisters—renders the prophetic cry of Isaiah ("Emmanuel... God with us" – Isa 7:14) into a direct appeal for Christ's coming (Veni, Veni, Maranatha). Gregorian chant manuscripts from the 9th century preserve antiphons for Advent that punctuate each verse with the acclamation, "Maranatha!"—invoking the bride's cry of Revelation 22:17. Martin Luther's chorales likewise adapted this theme; in his hymn *"Mit Fried und Freud ich fahr dahin"* he closes each stanza by looking forward to the "day of resurrection," a clear echo of Maranatha's dual tense promise (John 11:25–26). Composers such as Palestrina and Victoria set the word to soaring melismas during the Offertory, symbolizing the soul's ascending eagerness for the Bridegroom's arrival (Luke 12:35–36). Thus, from Roman basilicas to Lutheran kirchen, the melodic invocation of Maranatha became an aural bridge linking present worship to future consummation.

In the liturgical calendar, Maranatha finds its most pronounced resonance in Advent and on Christ the King (Last Sunday) observances. Advent collects often draw on Isaiah's plea, "O that You would tear open the heavens and come down" (Isa 64:1), followed by a congregational refrain of "Come, Lord Jesus" as the Gospel is proclaimed (Matt 24:44). The ongoing readings through Advent—such as Joel's call to "return to the LORD with all your heart" (Joel 2:12)—are framed by liturgical prayers ending in Maranatha, reminding the faithful that historical anticipation spills into personal repentance. On the final Sunday of the church year, when Revelation 22:20 is traditionally read, ministers pause after the line "He is coming soon," inviting the entire assembly to respond, "Amen. Maranatha!" This ritual link between proclamation and response transforms doctrinal confession into communal expectation. Even outside formal liturgies, many congregations recite the doxology in closing benedictions— "The grace of the Lord Jesus Christ... be with you all. Amen. Maranatha!" (Rev 22:21). In these appointed seasons, the church reclaims her ancient cry as both a corporate affirmation and a clarion call that, in God's perfect timing, our longing will be answered in full.

1.5 Reformation to Revival: "Come" through the Ages

1.5.1 Reformers' Emphasis on Christ's Return

The sixteenth-century Reformers reinvigorated the cry of Maranatha by insisting that Scripture alone, not ecclesial tradition, reveals Christ's eschatological promise. John Calvin, reflecting on 1 Thessalonians 4:16–17, argued that the assured bodily return of Christ ought to shape both the preaching of the pulpit and the daily life of believers. Martin Luther likewise taught that the believer "lives in the tension of the already and the not yet," urging congregations to cling to Romans 8:23's promise that we "wait for the adoption as sons, the redemption of our bodies." In his sermons on Christ's coming, Luther contrasted the deceptive security of indulgences with the genuine hope of Revelation 22:20, reminding hearers that only the Lord's return secures true salvation. The Magisterial Reformers embedded Maranatha into their catechisms—teaching children to pray daily, "Come, Lord Jesus, come!"—so that the next generation would inherit not mere moralism but living expectancy. They drew on Hebrews 10:25 to warn against forsaking "the assembling of ourselves together," since communal worship is itself a rehearsal of the heavenly gathering. Even amid political turmoil and church-state conflict, Reformed theologians held fast to the "blessed hope" (Titus 2:13), seeing in it both comfort under persecution and impetus for reform. Thus, from Geneva to Wittenberg, the Reformation sounded a clarion call that sharpened the church's longing for her returning Bridegroom.

1.5.2 Puritan "Blessed Hope" Sermons

In seventeenth-century England and New England, Puritan preachers built on Reformation foundations by making eschatology central to pastoral exhortation. Drawing repeatedly on Titus 2:13, they described the "blessed hope" as the chief incentive for holy living, preaching that "the earnest expectation of the creation" (Rom 8:19) ought to awaken slumbering souls. Thomas Goodwin's sermons on the Second Coming painted vivid courtroom scenes from Revelation 20, compelling congregations to examine their lives under the gaze of "the Judge of all the earth" (Gen 18:25). John Owen, in his monumental treatise *The Glory of Christ*, expounded Revelation 1:7, showing how "every eye" shall one day behold the King in glory, and urging believers to readiness lest the day "comes like a thief" (1 Thess 5:2). In New England's meetinghouses, the cry "Maranatha!" echoed through the long Psalm-singing services, reminding families that their true dwelling is in "the city with foundations" whose builder and maker is God (Heb 11:10). Puritan covenant renewal ceremonies often concluded with prayers imploring Christ's return to vindicate His people and fulfill the "new heavens and new earth" promise (Isa 65:17). Their emphasis on sanctification—"presenting every believer perfect in Christ"

18

(Col 1:28)—flowed directly from an eschatological vision that saw time as a sacred "day of salvation" (2 Cor 6:2). Through their fervent preaching, the Puritans bequeathed to later generations a robust "blessed hope" that fused doctrine with devotion.

1.5.3 Great Awakenings and Renewed Eschatological Fervor

The eighteenth and nineteenth centuries witnessed seismic revivals in Britain and North America, where preachers like Jonathan Edwards and George Whitefield rekindled the church's longing for Christ's return. Edwards's sermon "Sinners in the Hands of an Angry God" culminated in an appeal to "that great day" when the dead shall rise (John 5:28–29), sparking tears of repentance and a renewed sense of Maranatha. Whitefield's open-air preaching tours quoted Acts 1:11—"This same Jesus…will come in the same way"—urging multitudes to "watch and pray" as though the trumpet could sound at any moment (Matt 24:42–44). The Second Great Awakening further carried eschatological zeal into frontier camp meetings, where hymns such as "Lo! He Comes with Clouds Descending" filled the valleys with expectant praise (Rev 1:7). In the Wesleyan and Methodist circuits, preachers emphasized holiness as preparation for the Bridegroom's arrival, drawing on 1 John 3:3: "Everyone who has this hope purifies himself." These movements produced missionary societies convinced that taking the gospel "to every creature" (Mark 16:15) was both a Great Commission task and a harbinger of Christ's imminent return. The impact rippled into social reform—abolition, temperance, and education—driven by the conviction that "the kingdoms of this world have become the kingdoms of our Lord" (Rev 11:15). Thus, each wave of awakening renewed the church's eschatological fervor, proving that Maranatha is not merely a doctrine to be assented to, but an impulse that transforms worship, witness, and the whole trajectory of Christian history.

1.6 Living the Cry Today

1.6.1 Personal Devotion: Daily Prayer of Expectancy

Modern disciples can make Maranatha the heartbeat of their private devotions by weaving the cry "Come, Lord Jesus" into daily rhythms of prayer and Scripture meditation. Beginning each morning with Psalm 63's awakening plea—"O God, You are my God; earnestly I seek You; my soul thirsts for You…"—helps orient the heart toward the coming King (Ps 63:1). Before sleep, believers might echo the psalmist's cry, "My eyes are awake through the night watches, that I may meditate on Your promise" (Ps 119:148), reflecting on texts like Revelation 22:20. Journaling brief prayers of longing—"Maranatha, fill my heart with holy hope"—keeps eschatological anticipation alive, even amid routine tasks. Incorporating brief "arrow prayers" (one-sentence petitions) throughout the day—lifting up friends, communities, or global needs—anchors mundane moments in the tension of "already and not yet" (Col 3:1–4). By setting reminders on their phones or placing Maranatha-themed bookmarks in their Bibles, believers cultivate an attitude of watchfulness, embracing Paul's exhortation to "pray without ceasing" as a continuous invitation for Christ's presence (1 Thess 5:17).

1.6.2 Corporate Gathering: Cultivating "Maranatha" Communities

The local church can embody the ancient cry by structuring gatherings around expectant worship and mutual encouragement. Opening corporate services with Scripture passages such as Isaiah 64:1—"O that You would rend the heavens and come down"—followed by a congregational "Maranatha" response, reminds worshipers that every assembly foreshadows the heavenly banquet (Rev 19:9). Incorporating responsive readings of Revelation 22:17–20 and pausing after "He is coming soon" for the congregation to reply "Amen. Come, Lord Jesus!" transforms liturgy into living anticipation. Small groups and Bible studies can begin and end meetings with a moment of silence, inviting participants to center their prayers on Christ's return (Matt 24:42). Celebrating Communion with the mountaintop vision of 1 Corinthians 11:26—"For as often as you eat this bread... you proclaim the Lord's death until He comes"—deepens the sense that each Lord's Supper is an "earnest" of the feast to come. Churches that preach regularly on eschatological hope (1 Pet 1:3–5) and practice hospitality as a foretaste of the Marriage Supper of the Lamb (Rev 19:7–9) cultivate communities marked by both practical love and unwavering expectancy.

1.6.3 Mission as Missive: Proclaiming "Come" to All Nations

Living Maranatha means taking the cry beyond our walls as a gospel summons to the unreached. Empowered by Acts 1:8—"you will be my witnesses... to the ends of the earth"—missions teams can frame evangelistic efforts as invitations to participate in the Bridegroom's return. Preaching the Great Commission (Matt 28:19–20) with Maranatha as its eschatological horizon challenges churches to send and support cross-cultural workers who carry both word and deed ministries into resistant contexts. Short-term mission trips become more than service projects; they are living proclamations of the bride's call, sharing "the water of life" (John 4:14) in regions thirsty for truth. Digital missionaries and global partnerships can leverage social media and radio broadcasts to declare "Jesus is coming!" in hundreds of languages, echoing Revelation's universal invitation ("Whosoever will, let him take the water of life freely" – Rev 22:17). By integrating eschatological teaching into discipleship—training every believer to share not only the gospel of forgiveness but the hope of Christ's return—the church advances a mission that is itself a missive, inviting all peoples to stand ready before the throne and join the cry: "Maranatha! Come, Lord Jesus!"

Conclusion The cry "Maranatha—Come, Lord Jesus" has woven through centuries of Christian experience as both prayer and proclamation. We have seen it carved on tomb walls beneath Roman streets, chanted in Eastern liturgies, sung by medieval pilgrims, and preached by Reformers and revivalists alike. At every turn, it has served as a compass, directing the church's gaze away from temporal troubles toward the unshakeable promise of Christ's return.

Yet Maranatha does more than comfort the afflicted; it transforms how we live today. Our hope for the coming kingdom impels personal holiness, shapes corporate worship, and propels global mission. It calls us to hold fast in the face of apathy, to persevere under persecution, and to share the good news with urgency and compassion. By reclaiming this ancient cry in our own lives, we enter into the same expectancy that sustained the earliest believers—and we join in their song of hope.

As we journey forward through the chapters of this book, may Maranatha resonate in our hearts and hymns, guiding every step of faith. Let us pray with renewed intensity, serve with undimmed passion, and witness with steadfast courage—ever watchful, ever hopeful—for the day when heaven's doors swing open and our Lord appears. Come, Lord Jesus!

Chapter 2. The Sure Promise of Christ's Return

From the dawn of redemptive history, God has woven the promise of His Son's return into the fabric of His covenant dealings with humanity. That assured hope—anchored in the unbreakable word of Scripture—pierces the uncertainty of our present trials and infuses every moment with eternal perspective. As we survey the panorama of prophetic revelation, from Abraham's seed through the consummation of all things, one theme resounds above every other: Jesus Christ will come again. This chapter seeks to awaken our hearts to the steadfast certainty of that promise, not as a distant fairytale, but as a living reality that shapes how we pray, work, suffer, and worship today.

At its core, our confidence rests on the character of God, who neither slumbers nor changes, and on Christ Himself, who bore our sin, conquered death, and ascended victorious to prepare a place for us. His departure was not a farewell but a prelude to His triumphant return. Throughout the ages, faithful saints have clung to this "blessed hope," finding in it the strength to endure persecution, the courage to proclaim the gospel, and the motivation to pursue holiness. Here, we trace that historic trajectory—from the oracles of the prophets and the teaching of our Lord in the Upper Room, to the apostolic creeds and the creaking timbers of medieval cathedrals— discovering how every era has renewed its gaze heavenward.

Yet this promise is not confined to dusty scrolls or distant future speculation. It confronts us in our everyday decisions, calling us to live with hands ready, hearts undistracted, and eyes fixed on the unseen reality. Whether we face trials that tempt us to despair or comforts that lull us into complacency, the sure promise of Christ's return reorients our souls toward the eternal joy set before us. As we press into this truth, may we hear afresh the call of the Spirit and the Bride: "Come, Lord Jesus."

2.1 Prophetic Continuity

2.1.1 Abrahamic Covenant and Future Blessing

The promise given to Abraham in Genesis 12 stands at the foundation of all subsequent revelation concerning the coming of Christ. When God called Abram out of Ur and declared, "I will make of you a great nation" (Genesis 12:2), He also added, "and in you all the families of the earth shall be blessed" (Genesis 12:3). This universal dimension of the blessing points ahead to the Messiah, through whom Gentiles as well as Jews would receive salvation (Galatians 3:8). Abraham's faith was credited to him as righteousness (Genesis 15:6), setting a pattern for trusting in God's future fulfillment even when circumstances seemed impossible. Later, God reiterated and expanded this promise in the covenant of the pieces, assuring Abraham that his descendants would inherit the land (Genesis 15:18–21), foreshadowing the New Heavens and New Earth (Isaiah 65:17). In Romans 4, Paul underscores that believers inherit the same promise by faith, anticipating the ultimate blessing of resurrection life (Romans 4:13). The Abrahamic Covenant thus serves as both seed and pledge: seed in the physical descendants, and pledge in the spiritual seed, Christ (Galatians 3:16). Every prophetic oracle that speaks of a future king, restored kingdom, or coming age of peace flows from this primordial promise. When we long for Christ's return, we echo Abraham's hope—looking for city whose builder and maker is God (Hebrews 11:10). In this way, the Abrahamic Covenant roots our blessed hope in God's irrevocable word, reminding us that He is "able to do immeasurably more than all we ask or imagine" (Ephesians 3:20).

2.1.2 Davidic Throne: Forever Established

God's covenant with David in 2 Samuel 7 marks a decisive shift from a promise to a person. While Abraham's seed pointed ahead to the Messiah, David's throne provided the locus for His reign. The Lord told Nathan, "I will establish the throne of his kingdom forever" (2 Samuel 7:13), a promise echoed in Psalm 89:3–4 and reiterated by Isaiah (Isaiah 9:6–7). Though Israel's earthly kings would fail, the covenant ensured that the true King—Jesus Christ—would sit forever on David's throne (Luke 1:32–33). This everlasting aspect underscores the unshakeable nature of Christ's dominion, transcending every human regime. In Acts 2, Peter applies David's words to Jesus' resurrection and ascension, showing that David foresaw the Christ who would reign eternally (Acts 2:29–36). Throughout the prophetic books, the portrayal of the coming King in royal imagery—wearing priestly robes and executing righteous judgment—flows directly from this foundation (Zechariah 6:12–13). New Testament writers affirm that Jesus inherits David's throne by divine decree (Hebrews 1:8), and that every knee will bow before Him (Philippians 2:10–11). As we await His return, we do so not to crown a newcomer, but to acclaim the King who has been enthroned since eternity past (Revelation 5:12–14). Thus the Davidic Covenant anchors our hope in Christ's unending and righteous reign.

2.1.3 Major Prophets on the Day of the Lord

The "Day of the Lord" motif dominates the Major Prophets, casting both dread and hope over history's horizon. Isaiah opens his prophetic vision with a call to "Wail, for the day of the Lord is near" (Isaiah 13:6), yet later voices comfort to Zion, promising a new age of peace under her King (Isaiah 66:22–23). Jeremiah sees Babylon's doom and then envisions the restoration of Israel, as God "will bring them back to this place" (Jeremiah 30:3). Ezekiel portrays the valley of dry bones, symbolizing national resurrection and God's faithfulness to His scattered people (Ezekiel 37:1–14). In each case, the Day of the Lord comprises judgment on sin and salvation for the remnant. Zechariah, though often grouped among the Minor Prophets, likewise speaks of that Day when the Lord will go out "and fight against those nations" but then "will save His flock" (Zechariah 14:3–5, 9). The prophets thus prepare the way for the final Day, when Christ Himself—lamb-like and lion-like—will execute justice and usher in a new world (Revelation 6–19). New Testament authors interpret these passages Christologically, applying them to both first-century upheavals and the ultimate consummation (2 Peter 3:10; 1 Thessalonians 5:2). As we read the Major Prophets, we learn that the same hand that brings righteous wrath also extends mercy and renewal. The tension between judgment and hope echoes through Scripture until the day when "He will make the splendor of the Lord our God upon us" (Isaiah 60:2).

2.1.4 Minor Prophets and the Coming King

Though shorter in length, the Minor Prophets sound a clarion call to expect the King's arrival and live in readiness. Hosea laments Israel's unfaithfulness yet foretells a day when her children "shall come trembling from the west" and "return and seek the Lord" (Hosea 8:14; 11:10). Joel vividly portrays the outpouring of the Spirit and signs in sun and moon "before the great and awesome day of the Lord" (Joel 2:28–31), a passage Peter later cites at Pentecost (Acts 2:16–21). Amos warns of locusts and famine as preludes to divine judgment but also hints at restoration "after two days" (Amos 6:14), gesturing toward resurrection hope. Obadiah prophesies Edom's fall and Israel's uplifted walls, symbolizing vindication by the coming King (Obadiah 1:17). Jonah's sojourn in the fish's belly becomes a typology for Christ's death and resurrection (Matthew 12:40), underscoring God's power over death. Micah famously envisions a ruler "who shall shepherd My people" emerging from Bethlehem (Micah 5:2), fulfilled in Jesus' birth. Zephaniah speaks of a purified remnant who "shall trust in the name of the Lord" and dwell under His banner of love and faithfulness (Zephaniah 3:12–17). Haggai and Zechariah urge temple rebuilding but also point beyond to the glory yet to come (Haggai 2:6–9; Zechariah 4:6–10). Malachi closes the Old Testament with a promise that "the sun of righteousness shall rise with healing in His wings" (Malachi 4:2), sealing the prophetic canon with a note of radiant hope. Together, the Minor Prophets create a mosaic of expectation, inviting God's people to look beyond present woes to the King who will right every wrong.

2.2 Jesus' Olivet Discourse

2.2.1 Historical Setting and Audience

Jesus delivered the Olivet Discourse against the backdrop of a Jewish nation under Roman occupation and religious tension in Jerusalem. As He sat on the Mount of Olives overlooking the temple, His disciples marveled at its splendor and asked, "Tell us, when will these things be, and what will be the sign of Your coming?" (Matthew 24:3). This question reflects both skepticism and genuine longing among His followers. The temple's stones, destined for destruction, symbolized the fragility of earthly systems compared to the permanence of God's kingdom. Jesus' response bridges immediate events—like the siege of Jerusalem in AD 70—with the ultimate end of the age. By addressing false messiahs, wars, and natural disasters, He grounded His teaching in observable realities while pointing beyond them (Mark 13:5–8). The cultural milieu included Pharisaic and Sadducean debates, Hellenistic influences, and growing apocalyptic fervor, all of which shaped how His words were heard. His audience comprised primarily Jewish disciples but also interested pilgrims and curious onlookers drawn by His authority. They would carry these teachings into the early church, shaping its theology of the last things. Understanding this context helps us hear Jesus afresh—not as an abstract oracle but as a living voice calling a diverse audience to watchfulness. The urgency of His words is thus rooted in both first-century crisis and eternal destiny.

2.2.2 Signs of the End: Wars, Famines, Earthquakes

In Matthew 24, Jesus catalogues a sequence of distressing events—"You will hear of wars and rumors of wars...famine and earthquakes in various places" (Matthew 24:6–7)—that characterize both the present age and the period leading to His return. These "birth pains," as He later labels them (Mark 13:8), serve as indicators rather than precise timetables. History indeed bears witness to cycles of conflict, scarcity, and seismic upheaval, reminding us that the world remains fractured by sin. Yet such phenomena are also a divine messenger, calling humanity to repent and trust in God's sovereignty (Luke 21:28). The apostle Paul echoes this when he warns of "terrible times" in the last days, marked by moral decay and social unrest (2 Timothy 3:1–5). Natural disasters expose human vulnerability, driving some to despair and others to devotion. Earthquakes, in biblical symbolism, often herald theophanies—Moments when God breaks into history (Exodus 19:18; Revelation 6:12–14). Famines remind us of our dependence on God for every provision (Matthew 6:26–30), while wars reveal the futility of human attempts to establish peace apart from divine intervention. As we observe these signs, we must resist sensationalism and cultivate sober hope—recognizing that Christ's return brings justice and healing far beyond any earthly remedy. In this way, Jesus' warning transforms anxiety into anticipation, encouraging believers to stand firm amid turmoil.

2.2.3 Parable of the Fig Tree: Discernment

Immediately after listing global tribulations, Jesus tells the parable of the fig tree: "When its branch has already become tender and puts out its leaves, you know that summer is near" (Matthew 24:32). The fig tree, a familiar symbol of Israel and its spiritual condition (Hosea 9:10; Jeremiah 24:5–7), illustrates how careful observation leads to accurate interpretation of seasons. Just as budding leaves signal harvest time, the convergence of prophesied events indicates the nearness of Christ's coming. Discernment here requires spiritual sensitivity: Believers must distinguish between mere coincidence and covenantal fulfillment. False prophets and messiahs will abound (Matthew 24:24), making it imperative to test every claim against Scripture (1 John 4:1). Discernment also involves personal readiness; knowing the season does not substitute for holy living (Matthew 24:44). The parable thus balances knowledge with obedience—encouraging watchful readiness rather than speculative date-setting. Church history shows that misguided predictions breed disillusionment, but Scripture calls us to a wiser vigilance rooted in God's unchanging word (Numbers 23:19). In our time, as in every age, the fig tree parable reminds us that the Gospel's global advance and prophetic signs together testify to the Kingdom's arrival. By cultivating discernment, the church stands poised to greet her Bridegroom with confidence rather than confusion.

2.2.4 The Call to Watchfulness and Prayer

Following His teaching on signs and the fig tree, Jesus underscores the necessity of watchfulness and prayer: "Watch therefore, for you do not know on what day your Lord is coming" (Matthew 24:42). Watchfulness entails more than passive waiting; it implies active engagement in the present— living holy lives, serving the needy, and proclaiming the gospel. In Luke's parallel, Jesus depicts servants waiting for their master to return from a wedding feast, welcoming him at once if he comes unexpectedly (Luke 12:35–40). Prayer sustains this vigilance, aligning our hearts with God's will and strengthening us against spiritual lethargy (Romans 12:12). The early church practiced continuous prayer and fasting as part of their eschatological hope (Acts 1:14; 2 Corinthians 6:5). Through prayer, we join the Bride in longing for the Bridegroom (Song of Solomon 2:10) and participate in the outpouring of the Spirit (Joel 2:28–29). Watchfulness also fosters communal accountability, as believers encourage one another to remain steadfast (Hebrews 10:24–25). Jesus warns that complacency can lead to surprise and shame (Matthew 24:50–51), while prayerful expectancy yields joy and perseverance. Thus, watchfulness and prayer form the twin pillars of a life shaped by the sure promise of Christ's return.

2.2.5 "No One Knows the Day or Hour"—Trusting His Timing

Jesus concludes His Olivet teaching with a sober reminder: "But of that day and hour no one knows, not even the angels of heaven, nor the Son, but the Father only" (Matthew 24:36). By placing ultimate knowledge in the Father's hands, Christ guards against human presumption and date-setting. This divine secret underscores the transcendent wisdom of the Trinity and calls believers to trust God's sovereign timing. The unpredictability of His coming transforms every moment into an opportunity for faithful service (Matthew 25:1–13). Paradoxically, uncertainty fuels urgency: If we could pinpoint the hour, we might delay repentance or mission. Instead, the unknown day inspires constant readiness, as servants "do not know when the master of the house is coming" (Mark 13:35). The New Testament encourages believers to live as "children of light" (1 Thessalonians 5:5), sober-minded and awake, because the day will come like a thief (1 Thessalonians 5:2). Trusting His timing also sustains hope when delays provoke doubt (2 Peter 3:3–4). Peter responds by reminding us that God's "delay" is His patience, giving more time for repentance (2 Peter 3:9). Thus the hiddenness of the exact hour becomes a gift—inviting active faith, patient endurance, and joyous expectation rather than morbid speculation.

2.3 Apostolic Certainty

2.3.1 Peter's "Day Like a Thief" (2 Peter 3)

In his second epistle, Peter confronts scoffers who question the delay of Christ's return, writing, "Scoffers will come...saying, 'Where is the promise of His coming?'" (2 Peter 3:3–4). He reminds readers that God's redemptive timeline is not measured by human standards: "With the Lord one day is as a thousand years, and a thousand years as one day" (2 Peter 3:8). This perspective dissolves impatience into a broader view of divine faithfulness. When Christ does appear, it will be "like a thief," catching the unprepared by surprise and rewarding the vigilant (2 Peter 3:10). The imagery of a thief connotes both danger and stealth—warning that His coming will not follow predictable patterns. Peter's remedy for complacency is holiness and godliness, as believers "look for and hasten the coming of the day of God" (2 Peter 3:12). He emphasizes that this "new heaven and new earth" will be the culmination of creation's renewal (2 Peter 3:13). By coupling judgment with promise, Peter reinforces that certainty of return demands ethical transformation. His epistle thus offers pastoral exhortation: Live godly lives, sustain hope amid ridicule, and anticipate with joy the "day of God."

2.3.2 Paul's "Blessed Hope" (Titus 2:13) and "Meantime" Ethics

Paul exhorts Titus to teach sound doctrine, including the marking of lives by self-control and devotion "in the present age" as we await "the appearing of the glory of our great God and Savior Jesus Christ" (Titus 2:12–13). He calls this the "blessed hope," anchoring Christian ethics not in present rewards but in future consummation. This hope motivates believers to renounce ungodliness and live righteously, knowing our citizenship is in heaven (Philippians 3:20). Elsewhere, Paul urges the Thessalonians to "encourage one another and build one another up" as they await the Lord (1 Thessalonians 5:11). His teaching balances anticipation with practical responsibility: work honestly (2 Thessalonians 3:10–12), pray without ceasing (1 Thessalonians 5:17), and bear with persecutors (2 Timothy 3:12). The "meantime" becomes a classroom for faithfulness, where each action reflects the character of the coming King. Paul's letters thus fuse eschatology with ethics, showing that hope shapes conduct. In doing so, he testifies that the promise of Christ's return is not escapism but highest motivation for godly living under grace.

2.3.3 John's Vision in Revelation 19–22

The apostle John's apocalyptic vision culminates in a majestic portrayal of Christ's return and the eternal state. In Revelation 19, heaven rings with praise for the "King of kings and Lord of lords" riding on a white horse, judging and making war in righteousness (Revelation 19:11–16). This dramatic scene contrasts sharply with the "little while" of Revelation 2–3, where the churches are urged to endure trials (Revelation 2:10; 3:11). Chapters 20–22 depict the millennium, final rebellion, and the Great White Throne judgment, followed by the New Jerusalem descending out of heaven (Revelation 21:2). In this city, God dwells with His people, wiping away every tear (Revelation 21:3–4). John's vision makes tangible the promises of earlier revelation: a renewed creation, healed nations, and unbroken fellowship with God. Each image—sea no more, river of life, tree of life—echoes Eden while surpassing it in glory (Revelation 22:1–2). By ending with an invitation, "Come, Lord Jesus!" (Revelation 22:20), John emphasizes that the entire prophetic canon finds its climax in the Bride's longing for her Bridegroom. His vision thus undergirds apostolic certainty with vivid certainty.

2.3.4 Hebrews' Exhortation to "Strive for Full Assurance"

The author of Hebrews urges believers to "strive for full assurance of hope until the end" (Hebrews 6:11). Drawing on the faith hall of fame in Hebrews 11, he portrays men and women who died in faith without receiving the promised land, yet saw it from afar (Hebrews 11:13). Their example emboldens us to persevere, knowing that "God is not unjust to overlook your work and labor of love" (Hebrews 6:10). The discourse emphasizes the superior priesthood and sacrifice of Christ, assuring us that His intercession secures our entrance into the heavenly sanctuary (Hebrews 9:24). By reminding readers that "we have a sure and steadfast anchor of the soul" (Hebrews 6:19), the epistle connects hope with heavenly realities. This anchor enters the inner place behind the curtain, where Christ ever lives to make intercession (Hebrews 7:25). Thus, confident expectation is rooted in both God's character and Christ's high-priestly ministry. Through this pastoral appeal, the writer disciplines the community toward endurance and unwavering faith until the day dawns.

2.3.5 Early Church Creeds on the Parousia

From the Didache's admonition to watch and pray "lest you be found naked" in the coming day, to the Nicene Creed's affirmation that Christ "will come again in glory to judge the living and the dead," the early church codified apostolic certainty in concise declarations. These creeds distilled apostolic teaching into communal confession, safeguarding orthodoxy against heresy. The Apostles' Creed—though later formalized—reflects New Testament motifs: His descent into hell, resurrection on the third day, ascension to the right hand of the Father, and future coming to judge (Romans 14:9; Acts 1:11). By reciting these truths weekly, believers connected personal faith with the historic, global church. The creedal traditions thus ensured that every generation heard afresh the promise of His return, embedding it in liturgy and catechesis. Even councils, facing Christological controversies, affirmed the Son's eternal lordship and future advent, recognizing that any deviation threatened the very hope of Christians. In this way, the early creeds became vessels of apostolic certainty— handing down the sure promise as a living heritage for the church universal.

2.4 Patristic and Medieval Witness

2.4.1 Ignatius and the Imminence of Return

Ignatius of Antioch, writing in the early second century, emphasizes Christ's nearness with striking urgency. He exhorts believers to "be ready," reminding them that the Lord's return is at hand and that false teachers will seek to undermine the faith (Epistle to the Smyrneans, §6). For Ignatius, every gathering of the church serves as a rehearsal for the heavenly assembly, and he urges Christians to celebrate the Eucharist "in honest love" as a foretaste of the Marriage Supper of the Lamb (Revelation 19:9). He warns repeatedly against spiritual complacency, urging his readers to live as "living stones" built upon the cornerstone, Jesus Christ (1 Peter 2:4–6). His letters portray a church under persecution yet filled with hope, believing that present suffering is but a moment compared to the glory to come (Romans 8:18). Ignatius frames martyrdom itself as a pathway to meeting Christ face to face, echoing Paul's confidence that "to live is Christ, and to die is gain" (Philippians 1:21). His theological vision fuses imminent expectation with ecclesial unity, insisting that "where Jesus Christ is, there is the Catholic Church" (Epistle to the Smyrneans, §8). By anchoring hope in the living body of Christ, Ignatius prepares communities to endure trials with their eyes fixed on the returning King. His writings thus offer an early witness to the doctrine that the Son's coming "draws near" (James 5:8) even as history marches on.

2.4.2 Justin Martyr's Eschatological Apologetics

Justin Martyr, one of the first Christian apologists, defends the faith against pagan critiques by pointing to the fulfillment of Scripture in Christ's advent and promised return. In his *First Apology*, he argues that the Gospel's predictive prophecies—concerning a virgin birth (Isaiah 7:14), a suffering servant (Isaiah 53), and a future kingdom (Daniel 7)—validate the Christian proclamation (First Apology, §34). He then extends this logic to the eschaton, asserting that just as prophecies of Christ's first coming were fulfilled, so will those concerning His second coming and the final resurrection (Daniel 12:2). Justin portrays baptism as participation in Christ's death and future resurrection (Romans 6:3–5), linking present sacramental life with future hope. He also describes the Eucharist as a "medicine of immortality," looking forward to the day when believers share eternal life with the risen Lord (First Apology, §66). Addressing Roman authorities, Justin warns that their empire will pass away, but God's kingdom will endure forever (Daniel 2:44). His apologetic strategy thus weaves together historical evidence, prophetic fulfillment, and eschatological expectation into a coherent defense. By insisting that belief in Christ's return is not fanciful but grounded in divine revelation, Justin strengthens the church's resolve amid intellectual and political opposition. His work exemplifies how early Christians employed reasoned theology to uphold the "sure word of prophecy" (2 Peter 1:19) regarding the coming King.

2.4.3 Irenaeus on the Millennium

Irenaeus of Lyons, writing against Gnostic distortions in the late second century, affirms a literal thousand-year reign of Christ on earth (Revelation 20:1–6). He interprets the millennium as the restoration of creation, when the saints will reign "with Him a thousand years" after the resurrection of the righteous (Against Heresies, 5.32.1). For Irenaeus, this chronological period signifies more than symbolic hope; it vindicates God's justice by rewarding believers with participation in the world made new. He connects the millennium to the New Adam's redemptive work, showing how Christ recapitulates humanity's destiny (Romans 5:12–21). Irenaeus also emphasizes that the judgment of unbelievers and the binding of Satan precede this reign, demonstrating the triumph of divine sovereignty (Revelation 20:2–3). His exposition rejects spiritualizing tendencies, insisting that prophecy finds literal fulfillment in history's consummation. By rooting the millennium in both Old-Testament promises (Isaiah 65:25) and apostolic witness, Irenaeus secures the doctrine against allegorical erosion. His work reassures believers that God's timeline is purposeful, leading to a tangible era of peace and righteousness under Christ's kingship. In celebrating this hope, the church anticipates not merely a future state but the fulfillment of God's covenantal faithfulness across centuries.

2.4.4 Augustine's "Inaugurated Eschatology"

Augustine's City of God revolutionized eschatological thought by introducing an "already/not yet" framework for the Kingdom of God. He taught that Christ inaugurated His reign at Pentecost (Acts 2:1–4), establishing the heavenly city within the earthly one (Revelation 3:12). Yet he maintained that the fullness of this kingdom—marked by the resurrection of the body and final judgment—awaits the Son's return (1 Corinthians 15:51–52). Augustine's synthesis acknowledges the reality of spiritual renewal now while preserving future hope, mitigating extreme millenarian expectations. He draws on Jesus' teaching that "the kingdom of God is within you" (Luke 17:21) alongside promises of cosmic restoration (Romans 8:19–23). His vision shaped Western theology for a millennium, balancing social engagement with ultimate otherworldliness. Augustine's emphasis on the virtuous life as citizenship in the heavenly city encourages holiness "as children of light" while awaiting Christ (Ephesians 5:8). He also warns against date-setting and fanaticism, arguing that preoccupation with signs distracts from rightful love of God and neighbor (Matthew 24:36–44). In Augustine's hands, the church learns to celebrate Christ's reign now and trust His return later—an approach that still grounds contemporary eschatology in biblical tension.

2.4.5 Medieval Mystics: Yearning Beyond the Veil

Medieval mystics such as Bernard of Clairvaux, Hildegard of Bingen, and Julian of Norwich conveyed intense longing for Christ's return through visions and devotional writings. Bernard exhorted monks to "await the bridegroom" with the same vigilance as the virgins in the parable (Matthew 25:1–13), likening their lamps to a heart aflame with expectation. Hildegard's visionary poetry often placed her soul in dialogue with the returning Lord, describing ethereal choirs singing "Maranatha" above the stars. Julian of Norwich, reflecting on her revelation of Christ's wounds, found in His pierced hands the guarantee of resurrection life (John 20:27), which she extended to the promise of final restoration. These women and men experienced eschatological hope not as dry doctrine but as living encounter, a communion that transcended earthly suffering. Their mystical writings encouraged Christians to cultivate inner purity as preparation for the Bridegroom (Revelation 19:7–8). They also broadened the church's imagination, using symbolic language to make heavenly realities tangible to medieval hearts. While their era grappled with plagues, wars, and ecclesial abuses, these mystics pointed beyond temporal distress to the day when every tear would be wiped away (Revelation 21:4). Their voices remind us that the promise of Christ's return is as much a matter of the heart as of the mind—calling for contemplative stillness amid life's storms.

2.5 Reformation to Revival

2.5.1 Reformers' Stress on the Final Judgment

The sixteenth-century Reformers rediscovered Scripture's eschatological core, emphasizing Christ's return and the Last Judgment as central to saving faith. Martin Luther, in sermons on 2 Peter 3, declared that the doctrine of the Last Day kindles "a living and active faith" by reminding sinners of God's righteous wrath (2 Peter 3:7). John Calvin incorporated eschatology into his *Institutes*, affirming the resurrection of the body (1 Corinthians 15:52) and warning that Christ's coming will be both "joyful for believers and fearful for unbelievers" (Institutes III.25). The Reformers rejected medieval complacency that downplayed future judgment, restoring emphasis on accountability and final vindication (Romans 14:10–12). They argued that true assurance arises not from temporal prosperity but from conviction that Christ's atoning work secures us for the coming Day. Their preaching linked Reformation themes—justification by faith and the priesthood of all believers—to eschatological hope. By placing Christ's return at the center of worship and catechesis, they countered both antinomian license and undue legalism. This renewed focus prepared the ground for later revivals, as believers found in the future King the impetus for present reform. The Reformers thus bequeathed to the church a robust tension: live in holy reverence now, assured that final justice and mercy await when Christ appears.

2.5.2 Puritan "Looking for That Blessed Hope"

Puritan preachers in seventeenth-century England and New England made the "blessed hope" of Titus 2:13 a hallmark of their ministry. Richard Sibbes exhorted congregations to "set their affections on things above" (Colossians 3:2), cultivating holy life as evidence of readiness for the King's return. John Owen wrote extensively on the enjoyment of Christ in heaven, framing death as "a gracious arrest" that ushers believers into immediate presence with their Lord (2 Corinthians 5:8). Jonathan Edwards, though often remembered for his revival sermons, preached regularly on Christ's coming as the motive for godly living and missionary zeal. Puritan covenants and catechisms embedded eschatological questions—such as "What is the resurrection?"—into the fabric of family worship. They saw the Christian life as a pilgrimage toward the New Jerusalem, teaching children that "this world is not our rest" (Hebrews 13:14). Their emphasis on preparation led to the formation of "watchnight" services, gatherings on New Year's Eve that combined prayer, preaching, and communal watchfulness. The Puritans thus melded rigorous doctrine with vibrant devotional practice, showing that hope in Christ's return transforms daily piety into spirited anticipation. Their legacy endures in liturgies and spiritual disciplines that keep the Bridegroom's arrival ever before the church.

2.5.3 Great Awakening Preachers and Millennial Expectation

Eighteenth-century revivalists such as George Whitefield, Jonathan Edwards, and John Wesley preached with fervor about both personal conversion and the imminent arrival of Christ's kingdom. Whitefield's open-air sermons routinely drew thousands, as he summoned listeners to "prepare to meet your God" (Amos 4:12) in light of coming judgment. Edwards's famous sermon "Sinners in the Hands of an Angry God" vividly depicted the precarious fate of the impenitent, yet he balanced terror with the promise of mercy for those who repent (Joel 2:13). Wesley's Methodist societies practiced "watching" in small groups, fostering mutual accountability as they awaited the Second Coming. The Great Awakening thus linked revival fervor with eschatological urgency, framing missionary outreach as hastening the day when "all flesh shall see the salvation of God" (Luke 3:6). Preachers emphasized that signs of social upheaval and moral decay signaled the "last days," urging both personal holiness and societal reform. Revival societies maintained eschatological libraries, distributing tracts and books on prophecy and Christ's return. This period melded experiential religion with future-focused zeal, demonstrating that revival without eternity in view can wither into mere enthusiasm. The Great Awakening's millennial expectation continues to inspire modern revival movements to balance renewal with prophetic anticipation.

2.5.4 19th-Century Prophetic Movements

The nineteenth century witnessed a proliferation of prophetic societies and journals dedicated to interpreting current events through the lens of biblical prophecy. Leaders like Edward Irving and the Catholic priest Manuel Lacunza (writing under the pseudonym "Juan Josafat Ben-Ezra") popularized detailed timetables for Christ's return, drawing heavily on Daniel and Revelation. John Nelson Darby and the Plymouth Brethren systematized dispensationalism, positing a rapture of the church prior to a seven-year tribulation (1 Thessalonians 4:16–17). The *Scofield Reference Bible* further disseminated these ideas, making dispensational charts and notes ubiquitous in evangelical circles. Meanwhile, movements such as the Seventh-day Adventists emerged, emphasizing the imminent "investigative judgment" and the sanctity of the Sabbath (Revelation 14:6–7). Critics accused these groups of date-setting and sensationalism, yet their influence shaped the eschatological imagination of millions. Women's prophetic groups also arose, holding conferences on "Signs of the Times" to mobilize prayer and evangelism. Despite controversies, nineteenth-century movements reawakened interest in prophecy across classes and denominations. Their legacy persists in popular culture—from art and literature to film—and challenges the church to discern between healthy expectation and speculative excess.

2.5.5   20th-Century   Confessional   Statements   (e.g., Westminster, Lausanne)

In response to doctrinal fragmentation and millennial speculation, twentieth-century churches affirmed Christ's return in ecumenical confessions and declarations. The *Westminster Confession of Faith* (1646) and its Larger Catechism articulate the doctrine of the Last Judgment, the resurrection, and the beatific vision in sober, biblical language. Later, the *Lausanne Covenant* (1974) reaffirmed the church's commitment to proclaiming the gospel "with urgency" in light of Christ's return, linking evangelism, social responsibility, and discipleship. The *Barmen Declaration* (1934), while primarily addressing theological liberalism, implicitly upheld the eschatological hope as a guard against capitulation to worldly ideologies. In the Roman Catholic tradition, the *Second Vatican Council* (1962–65) restored an emphasis on "our glorious hope" (Titus 2:13) in its *Dogmatic Constitution on the Church (Lumen Gentium)*. These confessions emphasize that eschatology is not a fringe doctrine but integral to the church's identity and mission. By codifying essential beliefs, they help churches navigate contemporary challenges—such as secularism and interfaith dialogue—while maintaining a forward-looking hope. Their careful, Christ-centered formulations provide a stable foundation for congregations seeking to live in readiness without veering into sensationalism. In this way, twentieth-century statements continue the Reformation legacy of grounding doctrine in Scripture and tradition for the sake of faithful, hope-filled living.

2.6 Living in Expectant Confidence

2.6.1 Personal Holiness Motivated by His Coming

The certainty of Christ's return exerts a powerful influence on personal conduct, calling believers to pursue holiness as those who "love His appearing" (2 Timothy 4:8). Scripture repeatedly links eschatological hope with ethical exhortation: Peter writes, "Since all these things are thus to be dissolved…what sort of people ought you to be?" (2 Peter 3:11). Holiness, therefore, becomes not legalistic conformity but a joyful response to grace, reflecting the character of the One we anticipate (1 John 3:2–3). The apostle Paul urges believers to "put to death…what belongs to your earthly nature" (Colossians 3:5) in light of the transitory nature of this world (1 Corinthians 7:31). Early monastics practiced regular fasting, prayer, and Scripture meditation as disciplines to cultivate purity and readiness—anticipating Christ's visit like a bride preparing for her wedding. Modern spiritual writers call this "eschatological asceticism," a life rhythm shaped by both present devotion and future hope. Personal holiness thus integrates inward transformation with outward actions— compassion, integrity, and justice—demonstrating the kingdom now breaking into this age. As John Calvin observed, a living faith in Christ's return "puts wings on our good works," propelling us beyond duty into delight (Institutes III.25.2). In every choice—speech, relationships, stewardship—believers enact the values of the coming kingdom, bearing witness to a world yearning for redemption (Matthew 5:16).

2.6.2 Corporate Worship as a "Maranatha" Declaration

The gathered church embodies eschatological hope each time it meets, declaring "Maranatha" in word and sacrament. In the early church, believers "devoted themselves to the apostles' teaching and to fellowship, to the breaking of bread and to prayer" (Acts 2:42), anticipating Christ's presence among them (Matthew 18:20). Liturgy, hymnody, and preaching all converge to proclaim the story of redemption—from creation through cross, resurrection, and the promised return. The Lord's Supper enacts Christ's death until He comes, a tangible pledge of future fellowship at the heavenly banquet (1 Corinthians 11:26). Baptism likewise unites the believer with Christ in His death and resurrection, signaling participation in the age to come (Romans 6:4). Liturgical calendars mark Advent as a season of watchful longing, interspersing ancient "O Antiphons" that invoke the Messiah's advent with prayers for His return. Even doxologies—"To Him who sits on the throne and to the Lamb be blessing and honor and glory and might forever and ever!" (Revelation 5:13)—point beyond the sanctuary to heaven's ultimate worship. In contemporary services, responsive readings, prophetic art, and Christ-centered mission calls keep the horizon of His coming in view. By weaving eschatology into corporate rhythms, the church rehearses future reality now, proclaiming that the last word belongs to the One who is, who was, and who is to come (Revelation 1:8).

2.6.3 Mission and Evangelism as Foretaste of the Kingdom

Eschatological hope compels the church to share the gospel as a rehearsal for the Great Commission's consummation (Matthew 28:18–20). Every conversion is a foretaste of the new community gathered from all nations before God's throne (Revelation 7:9–10). Mission thus becomes an eschatological act: declaring freedom for captives (Luke 4:18), healing the sick, and calling the lost to repentance in anticipation of the coming King. Paul describes evangelism itself as "proclaiming this good news...in hope that...Christ will be magnified in my body" (Philippians 1:18–20). The global advance of the church signals to heaven and earth that the kingdom is making inroads amid present darkness (Colossians 1:13). Mission agencies historically have used prophecy conferences and evangelistic crusades to spur urgency, linking altar calls to the nearness of Christ's return. Modern practitioners speak of "kingdom advance" and "last-days harvest," framing cultural engagement as participation in divine restoration. This missional mindset resists both triumphalism and retreat, trusting that Christ's return vindicates sacrificial service. As leaders pray for "a great multitude...standing before the throne" (Revelation 7:9), they act on the conviction that the eschaton unfolds wherever Christ's name is lifted high.

2.6.4 Ethical Decision-Making in Light of the Parousia

Anticipating Christ's return shapes how believers navigate moral complexities, applying kingdom principles to issues of justice, technology, and public life. Scripture insists that "you know the time, that the hour has come for you to wake from sleep" (Romans 13:11), prompting decisions that reflect eternal rather than temporal values. In business, this may mean integrity over profit; in politics, truth over expediency; in science, stewardship over exploitation. The parables of the talents (Matthew 25:14–30) and the sheep and goats (Matthew 25:31–46) underscore accountability—our actions "in as much as you did it to one of the least of these" bear eternal weight. Ethical frameworks grounded in eschatology resist both moral relativism and escapist fatalism, fostering engagement that honors God and neighbor. Christian bioethicists, for instance, invoke the dignity of the resurrected body when addressing issues from genetic engineering to end-of-life care. Environmental ethics draw on the promise of a new earth (Revelation 21:1) to justify caring for creation now (Genesis 2:15). In every sphere, the knowledge that Christ will return as Judge and Redeemer informs choices, ensuring that our "yes" is yes and "no" is no (Matthew 5:37). Thus, eschatological hope becomes the lens through which complex decisions gain clarity and purpose.

2.6.5 Suffering with Hope: Patient Endurance in Trials

The sure promise of Christ's return sustains believers through affliction, transforming suffering into a context for grace and testimony. Peter exhorts Christians to "rejoice insofar as you share Christ's sufferings, that you may also rejoice and be glad when His glory is revealed" (1 Peter 4:13). The apostle Paul likewise counts present hardships "light and momentary" compared to the eternal weight of glory (2 Corinthians 4:17). Early martyrs, inspired by Hebrews 11, viewed death as "gain," confident that they would enter God's rest (Hebrews 4:9–10). Contemporary persecuted churches recite "Maranatha" as both prayer and creed, trusting that no amount of suffering can separate them from the love of God in Christ (Romans 8:35–39). The book of Revelation portrays the martyrs under the altar crying, "How long...?" only to receive the assurance that their number is complete before the hour of vindication arrives (Revelation 6:9–11). This vision reminds us that every tear and injustice is registered by the Lover of souls. Pastors counsel congregations that trials refine faith like gold tested by fire (1 Peter 1:7), producing endurance and character (Romans 5:3–4). Thus, the forward-looking hope of Christ's return anchors believers in storms, enabling them to bear witness to a world that needs both comfort and courage.

Conclusion

As we conclude our exploration of the certain return of our Savior, let us recall that this doctrine is not merely an abstract tenet but the heartbeat of Christian discipleship. The certainty of His coming transforms fear into faith, apathy into worship, and worldly striving into kingdom service. We stand on the shoulders of generations who have gone before, holding fast to that same unshakable hope, even as we await the final unveiling of our King.

May this truth reignite in us a renewed sense of urgency and joy—urgency to share the gospel with unreached souls, and joy in knowing that every tear will be wiped away when we stand in His glorious presence. Until that day dawns, let us walk in holiness, perseverance, and love, ever mindful that He who has promised is faithful. Our story does not end in the grave or the grave's shadow, but in the triumphant shout of resurrection life and unending fellowship with Christ our Lord. Maranatha—come, Lord Jesus, come.

Chapter 3. Signs in the Nations and the Cosmos

The tumult of our age—from geopolitical unrest to ecological upheaval and awe-inspiring celestial phenomena—often feels like a prelude to something greater than ourselves. Throughout history, God has spoken through the movements of nations and the rhythms of creation, calling His people to discern His hand at work even amid chaos. In this chapter, we will listen for the Lord's voice in the roaring of the seas and the stars fallen from their courses, in the rise and fall of empires and the heartbeat of every unreached people group. By attuning our spirits to these signs, we cultivate a deeper expectancy—not born of fear, but of faithful watchfulness—for the coming of our King.

Whether through quaking earth or shifting borders, through digital innovations that shrink distances or through the witness of brave believers in persecuted lands, these markers reveal both the brokenness of our world and the inexorable advance of God's redemptive plan. As we explore how the cosmos and the nations alike declare the glory of the Lord, may we learn to read the heavens and the headlines with eyes of hope, ever ready to proclaim, "Maranatha—Come, Lord Jesus."

3.1 Global Upheavals

3.1.1 Wars and Rumors of Wars

The Lord warned that "you will hear of wars and rumors of wars" as a hallmark of the last days, but He also reminded us not to be alarmed, for these things must first take place (Matthew 24:6). Throughout history, global conflicts have escalated in scale and intensity, from the world wars of the twentieth century to regional skirmishes that threaten wider conflagration. Each new theater of conflict—whether in Eastern Europe, the Middle East, or the South China Sea—resonates with Jesus' words, calling the church to discernment rather than despair. Empires rise and fall, yet human ambition remains constant, echoing the biblical pattern of power struggles (Daniel 2:21). Technology has multiplied the capacity for warfare—drones, cyber attacks, and long-range missiles—raising questions about how "wars...in various places" (Mark 13:8) prefigure the final shaking of nations. Ideological conflicts, often cast in religious or ethnic terms, further mirror the prophecies of "ethnos rising against ethnos" (Matthew 24:7), suggesting a swelling tide of mistrust and violence. Yet even amid these horrors, episodes of peacemaking and ceasefires hint at the ultimate Prince of Peace (Isaiah 9:6) who will one day halt all conflict. The apostle Paul assures us that God "has not destined us for wrath but to obtain salvation through our Lord Jesus Christ" (1 Thessalonians 5:9), reminding believers that they are called to be peacemakers in a warring world (Matthew 5:9). As Christians observe the headlines, they must pray for wisdom (James 1:5) and witness boldly, trusting that Christ's return will consummate the long-awaited reign of justice. In this way, wars and rumors of wars become both warning signals and invitations to intercede for peace.

3.1.2 Ethnic and Cultural Clashes

Jesus warned that "nation will rise against nation, and kingdom against kingdom" (Matthew 24:7), and few phenomena illustrate this better than the surge in ethnic and cultural tensions today. Mass migrations driven by conflict and climate change have reshaped demographics, often igniting backlashes that target vulnerable minorities. Such clashes—whether in refugee camps or urban centers—reveal humanity's struggle to live in peace under one God (Psalm 133:1). Historical grievances, old tribal animosities, and competing nationalisms all find fresh expression in modern politics. In some regions, religious identity is weaponized, resulting in persecution of believers (Hebrews 13:3) and echoing the Stoning of Stephen (Acts 7:58) more than two millennia ago. The Bible's vision of a multiethnic worshiping community (Revelation 7:9) contrasts sharply with these divisions, calling the church to embody reconciliation (2 Corinthians 5:18). Cross-cultural partnerships in missions and aid work offer glimpses of this envisioned unity, yet they also expose the depth of prejudice that still pervades human hearts (Romans 3:23). As believers engage in peacemaking, they testify to the power of the gospel to transcend ethnic barriers, fulfilling the promise that "In Christ there is no Jew or Greek" (Galatians 3:28). In every contested border and every disputed identity, the church is summoned to proclaim the peaceable kingdom of God and anticipate the day when "they shall beat their swords into plowshares" (Isaiah 2:4).

3.1.3 Economic Turbulence and Control

Economic crises—bank collapses, currency devaluations, crippling inflation—often precipitate social unrest and expose the fragility of systems built on human credit rather than divine provision. The book of James warns, "Come now, you rich, weep and howl for the miseries that are coming upon you" (James 5:1), reminding affluent societies that wealth hoarded in unjust ways will face God's scrutiny. In Revelation 13, the beast's enforcement of a "mark" for buying and selling (Revelation 13:16–17) resonates eerily with modern debates over digital currencies, biometric IDs, and cashless economies. Such technologies carry genuine benefits, yet they also prompt questions about surveillance, privacy, and the prophetic specter of economic control under an antichrist system. During the Great Depression and the 2008 financial crash, many believers saw in market collapses an echo of prophetic warnings, spurring renewed interest in biblical stewardship (Matthew 6:19–21) and communal care (Acts 2:44–45). Wealth disparity today—where a handful wield disproportionate influence—reflects the dire warning that "the labor of the righteous only spins a rope" for the unjust rich (Proverbs 13:23). Yet economic turbulence also creates openings for the gospel, as destitute populations become receptive to hope that transcends material prosperity (2 Corinthians 8:9). Churches that feed the hungry (Matthew 25:35) and teach financial wisdom incarnate the kingdom's values amid fiscal storms. Ultimately, economic control and calamity serve as both judgment and invitation—signals that the true King, not Mammon, will judge "the nations" and establish a reign of righteousness (Psalm 2:8–9).

3.2 Creation in Birth Pains

3.2.1 Earthquakes and Geological Disturbances

Jesus likened the end-time upheavals to birth pangs, saying that "there will be earthquakes in various places" (Matthew 24:7). Geological surveys confirm that seismic activity has intensified along major fault lines, from the Pacific Ring of Fire to the Eastern Mediterranean. In AD 33, an earthquake at Christ's death marked the world-changing event (Matthew 27:51); Revelation's opening seals unleash another series of earth-shattering judgments (Revelation 6:12–14). While plate tectonics explain the mechanics, Scripture assigns a deeper significance: God sometimes uses the shaking of creation to awaken human hearts to divine sovereignty (Exodus 19:18; Habakkuk 3:6). Modern disaster relief efforts—churches mobilizing to aid quake-victims—mirror the biblical call to bear one another's burdens (Galatians 6:2). Scientists and theologians alike see the groaning of creation (Romans 8:22) as both consequence of the Fall and harbinger of redemption.

Earthquakes remind us that even the ground beneath our feet is not ultimately under human control, pointing us instead to the Rock of Ages (1 Corinthians 10:4). When tremors strike, the church is called to proclaim that the same hand that shakes the hills also offers unshakeable refuge (Psalm 46:1–3). Thus, geological disturbances serve as divine drumbeats, calling creation—and its stewards—to long for the day when "there shall be no more death or mourning or crying or pain" (Revelation 21:4).

3.2.2 Climate Extremes and Environmental Decline

Jesus warned that famines would be among the signs of the end, and today we witness unprecedented climate extremes—droughts parch fields, storms ravage coastlines, wildfires consume forests, and floodwaters engorge rivers. The prophet Amos declared that God would "make the sun go down at noon and darken the earth in broad daylight" (Amos 8:9), images that resonate with modern reports of heat-waves and solar dimming from atmospheric particulates. Creation's groaning under the weight of exploitation (Romans 8:22) reveals both ecological crisis and spiritual opportunity: when famines hit, communities often listen to messages of hope more intently. In response to crop failures, many churches partner with sustainable-agriculture initiatives, embodying Genesis 2:15's call to steward the earth. Psalm 24 reminds us that "the earth is the Lord's and the fullness thereof," a declaration meant to fuel both worship and wise care. Climate activism, when grounded in biblical mandate, becomes an act of obedience to God's command to "till and keep" (Genesis 2:15). Yet environmental decline also reflects human rebellion and disconnect from Creator and creature alike. As believers engage in conservation, they witness to the coming renewal when "the desert shall rejoice and blossom like the crocus" (Isaiah 35:1). Thus, climate extremes function as birth pangs—painful reminders of a world under curse and hopeful indicators that the Redeemer's healing is on the horizon.

3.2.3 Epidemics and Global Health Crises

Throughout Scripture, plagues and pestilences are intertwined with divine judgment andcalls to repentance (Leviticus 26:25; 2 Samuel 24:15). In Luke 21:11, Jesus foretold "pestilences" alongside earthquakes and famines as birth throes of the age to come. The COVID-19 pandemic, Ebola outbreaks, and recurring influenza strains have exposed the fragility of global health systems, echoing biblical plagues yet also showcasing the ingenuity of medical science. Churches that opened their doors to serve as vaccination sites and support networks embodied the Body of Christ caring for the vulnerable (Matthew 25:36). Epidemics reveal social inequities—poor communities often suffer most—underscoring scriptural calls for justice and mercy (Proverbs 31:8–9; James 1:27). In Revelation 6:8, the pale horse carries Death and Hades, an image that reminds us of the Gospel's power to overcome even the most fearsome disease through Christ's conquering work (Revelation 1:18). Believers are called to pray for healing (James 5:14–16) and to proclaim the Good News of ultimate restoration: "By His stripes we are healed" (Isaiah 53:5). Epidemics can drive people to despair or to the foot of the cross; the church's faithful witness in pandemics serves as a sign of the world-renewing Kingdom that is already breaking in. In every hospital ward and isolation unit, the promise of Christ's return casts a hopeful light upon suffering and reminds us that death will one day be swallowed up in victory (1 Corinthians 15:54).

3.3 Cosmic Portents

3.3.1 Solar and Lunar Phenomena

Joel's prophecy declares, "The sun shall be turned to darkness, and the moon to blood, before the great and awesome day of the Lord comes" (Joel 2:31). Modern observers note solar eclipses and blood-red lunar eclipses, phenomena that have inspired awe and dread across cultures. Jesus alluded to these portents, saying that "the sun will be darkened, and the moon will not give its light" before the Son of Man appears (Matthew 24:29). Today's scientists explain eclipses in astronomical terms, yet the Bible invites us to read the heavens devotionally, as canvas upon which God paints prophetic strokes (Psalm 19:1–2). Historically, eclipses have coincided with significant upheavals—emperors falling, battles won or lost—encouraging both pagan and Christian interpreters to see divine messages in celestial shadows. In the early church, believers commemorated such events as reminders of Christ's sovereignty over sun and moon (Colossians 1:16). Contemporary pastors often incorporate eclipse imagery in sermons on Christ's return, linking physical darkness with spiritual vigilance (Mark 13:35–37). While we resist superstition, we neither dismiss the Bible's teaching that creation itself will signal the approaching Day of the Lord. Every eclipse calls the church to lift its gaze upward—not to astrology but to the One who hung the stars in place (Genesis 1:16; Jeremiah 31:35)—and to pray, "Maranatha—Come, Lord Jesus" (Revelation 22:20).

3.3.2 Stars, Meteors, and Comets

Scripture portrays stars both as fixpoints in God's order and as harbingers of cosmic disturbance. Jesus said that "the stars will fall from heaven" (Matthew 24:29), an Image that evokes meteor showers and fireballs streaking through the sky. The book of Revelation describes a great star named Wormwood turning waters bitter (Revelation 8:10–11), a vivid metaphor for spiritual deception or environmental disaster. In ancient times, comets and shooting stars were often viewed as omens of major events, and even today they capture global attention, prompting reflection on human frailty and divine majesty. Modern astronomers track near-earth objects for planetary defense, yet the biblical vision reminds us that these celestial bodies are under God's authority (Psalm 148:3–6). The Magi's journey to worship the newborn King under a "star" (Matthew 2:2) foreshadows how signs in heaven both announce and herald divine action in human history. Meteoroid impacts and cosmic dust also shape our world, reminding us of creation's dynamic nature. While sensational headlines may ascribe apocalyptic meaning to every meteor sighting, Scripture calls us to sober discernment (1 John 4:1) and to keep our hope anchored in the unchangeable Word (Hebrews 1:10–12). Each blaze across the night sky, then, testifies to the Lord's creative power and beckons us to await the final unveiling of "the glory of our great God and Savior Jesus Christ" (Titus 2:13).

3.3.3 Auroras, Lights, and Unexplained Skies

Northern and southern lights—auroras shimmering in greens, purples, and reds—have long been sources of wonder and cultural myth, yet for Christians they can be a reminder that God paints the heavens with prophetic purpose (Psalm 97:6). Although auroras result from solar wind interacting with Earth's magnetosphere, the Bible tells us of "wonders in the heavens above" that will accompany the Lord's return (Luke 21:11). Unsought aerial phenomena—flashes of strange lights or unexplained atmospheric glows—often spark speculation about UFOs or supernatural forces. Discernment is crucial: Scripture warns against seeking signs for their own sake (Matthew 12:39) yet affirms that God may use unusual phenomena to draw our attention to Himself. Medieval chroniclers recorded "fiery crosses" and "celestial swords" as divine portents, much as today's news outlets document mysterious sky-shows. The church's task is neither to sensationalize nor to dismiss out of hand, but to test every experience by the Spirit and the Word (1 Corinthians 2:14–16). When Christians witness unexplained lights, they should pray for clarity—asking if God is nudging us toward repentance or renewed awe. At the same time, we should not neglect more ordinary signs of His presence, such as Scripture's daily reading (Psalm 119:105). In balancing wonder with wisdom, the church can use these sky-bound miracles as springboards for gospel conversation, inviting seekers to look beyond the cosmos to the Creator who declared, "Let there be light" (Genesis 1:3).

3.4 Digital Age as Sign

3.4.1 Global Connectivity and the Gospel

The advent of the internet and mobile technology has effectively fulfilled Jesus' prophecy that the gospel would be preached "to all nations" before the end comes (Matthew 24:14). Platforms like social media, video streaming, and messaging apps enable believers to share Scripture, testimonies, and worship songs across continents in seconds. Online translation tools have opened doors in regions where physical Bibles are scarce, echoing Isaiah's vision that "to the coastlands far away the LORD said, 'You shall bring them,' even the children of the dispersed" (Isaiah 49:1). Virtual prayer rooms and live-streamed church services create spiritual communities that transcend geographical barriers, embodying Paul's declaration that "in Christ you are being built together into a dwelling of God by the Spirit" (Ephesians 2:22). Digital connectivity also brings unparalleled opportunities for discipleship: worldwide Bible reading plans, interactive theology courses, and mentoring via video calls. Yet this connectivity carries responsibilities: online evangelism must be coupled with genuine pastoral care to avoid superficial engagement (James 2:17). Cyber outreach initiatives have spurred mass conversions—sometimes thousands in a day—showing how digital "ends of the earth" are being reached in real time (Acts 13:47). At the same time, the church must guard its witness against the pitfalls of digital sensationalism, ensuring that digital platforms amplify Christ's voice rather than human vanity (1 Corinthians 10:31). Ultimately, global connectivity signals that the harvest is ripe and equips the church to labor in unity until the Master reaps through His return (John 4:35).

3.4.2 Surveillance, Big Data, and the Mark

Rapid advances in data collection—facial recognition, biometrics, and centralized databases—have raised ethical alarms about privacy and control, evoking Revelation's warning that "no one may buy or sell except one who has the mark" (Revelation 13:17). While many of these technologies offer practical benefits—fraud prevention, improved security, personalized services—they also tempt societies toward intrusive surveillance states. Biblical teaching underscores the value of personal dignity and freedom: every human bears God's image (Genesis 1:27) and deserves respect and autonomy. When data giants or governments amass comprehensive digital profiles, the potential for manipulation—commercial, political, or even religious—grows exponentially. Some theologians see in these trends a foreshadowing of end-time systems that demand allegiance in exchange for participation in daily life (Daniel 3:16–18). The church must discern when legitimate technological progress crosses prophetic lines, advocating for transparency and ethical safeguards (Proverbs 29:2). At the same time, believers should resist dystopian fatalism, trusting that Christ alone holds ultimate authority over every system (Colossians 1:16–17). Christian technologists and ethicists are called to develop frameworks that honor both innovation and human flourishing, modeling the kingdom's values in code and policy. As we navigate the age of big data, our prayer must be that God's truth—not algorithms—guides hearts, preparing a people ready to worship without coercion when the Lamb appears (Revelation 7:15).

3.4.3 Information Overload and Discernment

The digital revolution has ushered in an era of unprecedented information flow: news alerts, social feeds, podcasts, and online articles bombard us at all hours. Paul's admonition to "test everything; hold fast what is good" (1 Thessalonians 5:21) has never been more relevant. Misinformation, deepfakes, and sensational clickbait can distort truth and sow confusion, echoing Peter's warning that "there will be false teachers among you" (2 Peter 2:1). The church must equip believers with discernment tools—sound hermeneutics, theological literacy, and critical thinking skills—to navigate this "noise." Sunday schools and small groups can teach media discernment alongside biblical doctrine, helping Christians recognize bias and cross-check sources (Proverbs 18:13). Spiritual disciplines—solitude, scripture meditation, and prayer—anchor us when the digital tide threatens to overwhelm (Psalm 119:105). Yet the same channels that propagate falsehood also offer avenues for truth: viral testimonies, livestreamed sermons, and global prayer networks. When harnessed wisely, information networks become instruments of the Spirit's work, echoing John's charge to "write...the things that you have seen" (Revelation 1:19) for every generation. As the digital frontier expands, the church's calling is clear: be a trustworthy filter, guiding seekers to the immutable Word amid ever-shifting data. In doing so, we testify that the ultimate revelation is not an algorithm but Christ Himself, the Word made flesh (John 1:14).

3.5 Gospel Witness to All Peoples

3.5.1 Unreached Ethne and the Great Commission

Jesus commanded His followers to make disciples of "all nations" (Matthew 28:19), and global research identifies some 7,000 distinct people groups yet to hear a clear gospel presentation. These remaining "ethne" often dwell in remote regions, protected tribes, or closed societies. Mission organizations now employ drone-delivered scriptures, solar-powered audio Bibles, and contextually translated multimedia evangelism to penetrate barriers of geography, language, and literacy. This regional focus fulfills Isaiah's promise that "the coastlands shall wait for His instruction" (Isaiah 42:4), as the gospel extends from urban centers to forgotten villages. Indigenous-led church planting movements demonstrate that locals trained in theology and pastoral care can multiply generations of disciples more effectively than external missionaries alone. At the same time, prayered mapping initiatives—where every ethne is paired with a prayer group— keep the church's intercession aligned with global need (Colossians 4:3). Though challenges like persecution, natural disasters, or political interference impede progress, technological innovations and a renewed commitment to partnership are accelerating the pace. As the harvest grows, the urgency intensifies: every coin flip of history's clock brings us closer to the day when every tribe and tongue will worship before God's throne (Revelation 7:9). The church's perseverance in reaching unreached peoples thus becomes both sign and agent of the kingdom's advance.

3.5.2 Persecution and Perseverance

In many regions, the gospel advances most powerfully through suffering and witness under pressure. Jesus warned His disciples that they would be "hated by all nations for My name's sake" (Matthew 24:9). Today's global watch lists document hundreds of thousands of believers imprisoned, tortured, or martyred annually. Yet persecution often fuels faith rather than extinguishing it: the underground church in nations hostile to Christianity has seen rapid growth, testifying to Paul's words that "a great door for effective work has opened to me" even in chains (2 Corinthians 2:12–13). Martyrs' testimonies—like those under the altar in Revelation 6:9–11—cry out for justice and inspire global empathy. Networks that smuggle Bibles, train house-church leaders, and provide relief to persecuted families embody Christ's compassionate love (Matthew 25:40). The international church rallies during global observances—like the International Day of Prayer for the Persecuted Church—reminding believers in the West that freedom must be used to pray, give, and advocate. Psychological studies reveal that persecuted Christians often display higher levels of joy and resilience, illustrating Paul's paradox: "Rejoice...for you share in the sufferings of Christ" (1 Peter 4:13). Their perseverance shines as a prophetic witness, signaling that the kingdom triumphs in weakness. In standing with them, global believers affirm that the cost of discipleship is worth the ultimate reward at Christ's appearing (2 Timothy 4:8).

3.5.3 Mass Movements and Revival Waves

History's great revivals—such as those under Wesley, Whitefield, and the Welsh Revival of 1904–05—have served as foretaste of the eschatological harvest, igniting mass conversions and social renewal. Contemporary movements in sub-Saharan Africa, Southeast Asia, and South America report millions coming to Christ within years, often through house-church and cell-group strategies. These "people movements" demonstrate that when the church prays fervently and preaches faithfully, barriers of caste, tribe, and language collapse (Galatians 3:28). Signs and wonders—healings, liberations, prophetic words—often accompany such waves, affirming the kingdom's presence (Mark 16:17–18). Strategic cooperation between denominations and parachurch organizations ensures that new believers receive discipleship and local pastoral oversight, preventing shallow faith. Digital platforms enable global prayer coverage for these movements, linking intercessors in North America or Europe with pastors in unreached regions. Scholars note that mass movements frequently correlate with periods of social upheaval—political transitions, economic crises—echoing the birth-pain dynamic (Luke 21:26). As revival spreads, it creates momentum that can shift national trajectories, fostering moral reform and community development. Ultimately, each wave of awakening points toward the final ingathering when Christ returns for His Bride, clothing her in righteousness (Revelation 19:7–8).

3.6 Eschatological Geography

3.6.1 Jerusalem at the Center

Scripture repeatedly returns to Jerusalem as prophetic fulcrum—for blessing or judgment—culminating in Zechariah's vision that "the LORD will go forth and fight against those nations" and "the LORD will be king over all the earth" (Zechariah 14:3, 9). Today, Jerusalem remains a focal point of geopolitical tension, religious pilgrimage, and prophetic expectation. Jewish, Christian, and Muslim claims intersect around its holy sites, making it a microcosm of worldwide spiritual conflict. Pilgrims trek to its walls, praying in the Garden of Gethsemane or before the Western Wall, embodying Psalm 122's call to "pray for the peace of Jerusalem." Modern Israeli government decisions—recognizing Jerusalem as capital, expanding settlements—spark international debate, leading some to see unfolding prophecy in real time. Yet the New Testament reframes true

Jerusalem as both a present spiritual reality and a future heavenly city (Galatians 4:26; Revelation 21:2). The church's eschatological imagination should thus balance concern for earthly justice with trust in God's ultimate plan—knowing that He will restore Zion and draw all nations to Himself (Isaiah 2:2–3). Intercessors around the globe continue to pray for Jerusalem's peace and for the gospel to find deep roots among its diverse inhabitants. In doing so, they anticipate the day when Christ, the true King of Zion, will reign from Jerusalem and all nations will stream to His throne (Psalm 72:11).

3.6.2 Rivers, Seas, and Desert Regions

Biblical prophecy frequently employs geographic features—rivers as boundaries, seas as barriers, deserts as testing grounds—to convey spiritual truths about the last days. Revelation 16's sixth bowl dries up the Euphrates to prepare the way for the kings of the east, symbolizing geopolitical shifts and the exposing of hidden powers (Revelation 16:12). Contemporary dam projects and water scarcity in Middle Eastern regions bring fresh relevance to these images, revealing how control of water resources can spark conflict and prophetic reflection. The "four corners of the earth" (Revelation 7:1) include deserts like Sinai and Arabia, historically places where God met His people in solitude and trial (Exodus 3:1; 1 Kings 19:4–8). Today, desert regions host missions to nomadic tribes, using solar-powered audio devices to share Scripture where traditional outreach is impossible. Coastal megacities rising on reclaimed land evoke Genesis' promise that "sea and its waves roar" before the Lord (Psalm 98:7), reminding us of creation's dynamic response to its Maker. Christian relief efforts that bring clean water to drought-stricken communities enact prophetic mercy, prefiguring the river of life flowing from the throne (Revelation 22:1). By tracing these geographic markers, believers see how prophetic motifs play out on modern maps—energizing intercession, mission strategy, and hope for God's ultimate triumph over every river, sea, and desert.

3.6.3 Global Cities and Babylon Imagery

The apostle John's vision of "Babylon the great" (Revelation 17:5) portrays an economic and cultural powerhouse whose decadence provokes divine judgment. In our era, global cities—financial centers like New York, London, Shanghai—mirror Babylon's influence: hubs of commerce, media, and ideologies that shape the world. Skyscrapers gleaming by night evoke Babylon's grandeur, while underlying social ills—poverty, exploitation, moral relativism—reveal the city's shadow side. Revelation 18 depicts merchants mourning Babylon's fall, lamenting the loss of luxury goods—a vivid depiction of economic collapse and its moral implications (Revelation 18:11–13). Contemporary Christians living in or ministering to such cities must navigate the allure of materialism and the challenge of proclaiming an alternative kingdom. Urban mission movements—church planting, marketplace chaplaincy, arts outreach—aim to establish pockets of the New Jerusalem within these sprawling metropolises (Hebrews 12:22). The prophetic call to "come out of her" (Revelation 18:4) does not necessarily demand physical relocation but warns against complicity in systems that oppress. As Christ's ambassadors in global cities, believers serve the least, uphold justice, and model the city whose gates are never shut (Psalm 24:7–10; Revelation 21:25). In this way, urban ministry becomes a foretaste of the world redeemed—a sign that Babylon's reign will end and every knee will bow at the Lamb's appearing (Philippians 2:10).

Conclusion

As we conclude our survey of the signs unfolding in both earth and sky, it becomes clear that every groan of creation and every stirring of humanity points toward the climactic return of Christ. These portents are not to be parsed for date-setting or sensational headlines, but to awaken our hearts to sober expectation and active engagement. In recognizing the fingerprints of the Almighty on global events and cosmic wonders alike, we are invited to join in His work: proclaiming the gospel to all nations, caring for creation, and standing in prayerful solidarity with those who bear witness under trial.

Ultimately, the tapestry of signs in the nations and the cosmos serves a single purpose—to prepare a people who live in holy urgency and joyful anticipation. Let these revelations sharpen our discernment, deepen our compassion, and fuel our mission, as we lift our voices together in the ancient cry: "Come, Lord Jesus, come."

Chapter 4. The Great Apostasy and the Faithful Remnant

In every age the church has faced the twin currents of compromise and conviction—forces that either erode its witness or refine its faithfulness. As we approach the climax of history, Scripture warns that many will abandon sound teaching, trading the life-giving truth of the gospel for diluted comforts or seductive errors. Yet even in periods of widespread backsliding, God preserves a believing remnant—those whose hearts remain tethered to Christ and whose lives bear the marks of His Spirit. This chapter explores how the drift away from biblical fidelity manifests in doctrine, devotion, and discipline, and how, amid that apostasy, a countercultural community endures, testifies, and points forward to God's final triumph.

Our journey moves from the subtle allure of half-truths and cultural capitulation to stories of steadfast saints, both ancient and modern, who stood firm when tides turned against them. As we trace the contours of decline and the contours of hope, we discover not only the sobering reality of falling away but also the powerful assurance that God's purposes cannot be thwarted. In the tension between apostasy and remnant, we find both warning and encouragement: a call to vigilance and a promise of preservation.

4.1 Doctrinal Drift in the Last Days

4.1.1 Subtle Heresies and Half-Truths

The infiltration of error often begins not with outright denial of Christ, but with the mingling of worldly philosophies into gospel preaching, resulting in a message that tickles ears rather than transforms hearts (2 Timothy 4:3). Such blending can take the form of prosperity teaching, which elevates health and wealth above the cross, subtly shifting the focus from grace to gimmicks (1 Corinthians 1:17). Likewise, moral relativism, which denies absolute truth, undermines the very foundation of God's Word by asserting there are no fixed standards for right and wrong (John 17:17). The "Jezebel" spirit that tolerates false teaching in Thyatira illustrates how charismatic gifts can mask doctrinal corruption, as love for truth gives way to appetite for tolerance (Revelation 2:20–21). Early church councils combated similar half-truths by articulating the full person and work of Christ, yet today many pulpits shrink from historic creeds for fear of offending modern sensibilities (Hebrews 13:9). When even small compromises go unchecked—such as downplaying sin or ignoring Christ's exclusivity—they pave the way for deeper apostasy (Galatians 1:6–9). Believers must therefore guard the deposit of faith entrusted to them, "contending for the faith once for all delivered" (Jude 1:3). Discernment requires familiarity with Scripture's whole counsel so that any deviation from apostolic teaching is recognized and rebuked (Acts 20:27–28). In this way, the church can resist the subtle drift toward diluted gospel and remain anchored in truth.

4.1.2 Creeping Secularism and Spiritual Apathy

Secularism's advance into Western culture has recast Christianity as just another private opinion, removing faith's public voice and relegating God's Word to the margins of policy and education (2 Timothy 3:1–5). This "cultural Christianity" appears robust on the surface—church buildings, festivals, and Sunday attendance—but is hollow at its core when conviction and obedience to Scripture are absent (Matthew 7:21–23). As entertainment and technology press in, many believers find their spiritual hunger anesthetized by distraction, substituting screen time for soul care (Psalm 119:37). The decline of biblical literacy compounds the problem: if the majority cannot locate core doctrines in their Bibles, they cannot defend them (Romans 10:17). Meanwhile, public schools and universities increasingly dismiss supernatural realities, teaching that moral behavior is merely social convention (Romans 1:18–25). Churches that seek political alliances or social relevance at the expense of prophetic witness risk becoming indistinguishable from the world they once called to repentance (Amos 5:24). To counteract apathy, congregations must reclaim spiritual disciplines—regular fasting, focused prayer, and communal Scripture reading—to foster genuine hunger for God's presence (Matthew 6:16–18; Acts 2:42). Lay leaders should be equipped to model vibrant faith in everyday contexts, demonstrating that secular roles (workplace, family, civic life) are arenas for gospel witness (Colossians 3:23–24). Only as believers awaken from spiritual slumber can the church recapture its first-century vitality and withstand the tide of secular indifference.

4.1.3 Institutional Compromise and Power Plays

Throughout history, the church has sometimes traded its prophetic voice for political favor, forging alliances that compromise its allegiance to Christ (Matthew 22:21). When ecclesial bodies seek government patronage or economic leverage, they risk subverting the gospel's emancipating power, becoming instruments of the state rather than agents of transformation (Acts 5:29). The prophet Amos lamented when Israel's religious leaders "melted the righteous" in pursuit of societal approval rather than defending justice (Amos 2:6–7). In more recent centuries, some denominations have muted calls for holiness to protect denominational revenue or membership numbers (Revelation 3:15–16). Ecclesiastical power plays—clericalism, hierarchical control, and resource monopolization—can stifle lay initiative and distort the priesthood of all believers (1 Peter 2:9). Accountability structures such as plural eldership, transparency in finances, and external review boards serve as biblical guardrails against these tendencies (1 Timothy 3:1–13). Renewal movements often arise from grassroots frustration with top-down compromise, reminding institutional leaders that true reform comes from repentant hearts rather than corporate maneuvers (2 Chronicles 7:14). Awareness of this history equips today's church to resist the temptation to blend into the surrounding culture for comfort, preserving its distinct calling to bear prophetic witness—even if that means standing alone (Hebrews 10:32–34). Ultimately, the church's legitimacy rests not on its worldly power but on its fidelity to the gospel of Christ crucified and risen (1 Corinthians 1:18).

4.2 Signs of Apostasy in Practice

4.2.1 Moral Decline and Social Conformity

As society redefines marriage, the sanctity of life, and core moral categories, churches face mounting pressure to conform or appear intolerant (Romans 12:2). Cultural shifts often outpace theological reflection, leaving some congregations capitulating to prevailing norms rather than upholding biblical mandates on sexuality and justice (1 Corinthians 6:9–11). The redefinition of marriage in many nations challenges the church to articulate the creational basis for male–female union (Genesis 2:24) and to offer compassionate pastoral care without compromise (Ephesians 4:15). When Christians adopt prevailing values on life issues—abortion, euthanasia, genetic design—they undermine their prophetic credibility (Psalm 139:13–16). The apostle Paul's exhortation to "not be conformed to this world" (Romans 12:2) remains a clarion call for all believers to resist moral relativity, choosing obedience to Christ above social acceptance. Courageous dissent, modeled by Daniel refusing to bow to the statue in Babylon (Daniel 3), inspires present-day believers to endure ridicule rather than abandon conscience. Church bodies that remain silent on moral hotspots sow confusion among younger generations, who see no difference between Christ's ethics and cultural compromise (Matthew 5:13). Yet churches that uphold Scripture's teachings with humility and grace can demonstrate that obedience to God's design leads to genuine flourishing, even when it runs counter to societal currents (John 8:31–32). The tension of moral decline thus becomes a catalyst for renewed discipleship, calling the faithful to embody Christ's countercultural way.

4.2.2 Worship Without Holiness

When worship gatherings prize emotional experience over doctrinal substance, they risk devolving into spectacle rather than sacrament (Isaiah 29:13). Charismatic music, multimedia effects, and theatrical lighting can engage the senses, but if the Word is sidelined, participants leave entertained rather than equipped for transformation (2 Timothy 3:16–17). Seeker-sensitive models, aiming to remove barriers for unchurched attendees, sometimes dilute essential doctrines to avoid offense, inadvertently hollowing out the gospel (Galatians 1:6). True worship engages both heart and mind, integrating biblical preaching, communal confession, sacramental observance, and Spirit-led prayer (John 4:23–24). Historic liturgies—with responsive readings, creeds, and sacramental rhythms—guard against improvisation that may drift into relativism, anchoring congregations in centuries of orthodox practice (1 Timothy 4:13). The recovery of Word-centered liturgy reorients worshipers around Christ's story, reminding them that worship is first and foremost about God's actions, not human emotions (Revelation 5:9–10). Pastors and worship leaders bear responsibility to ensure that every element—music, sermon, ritual—points beyond self-fulfillment to the triune God (Psalm 100:2). Education in congregational singing, biblical theology, and spiritual formation equips participants to engage worship actively, preventing passive consumerism (Hebrews 10:24–25). In this way, worship without holiness is transformed into gatherings that both honor God and shape lives of obedience.

4.2.3 Leadership Failures and Scandals

When shepherds abuse authority—through financial misconduct, moral failure, or authoritarianism—they damage not only individual souls but the church's entire witness (Ezekiel 34:2–4). High-profile scandals draw media attention, leaving laypeople disillusioned and seekers skeptical of Christianity's claims (John 13:35). Yet accountability measures—plural eldership, regular audits, and external oversight—reflect biblical precedents for mutual correction (1 Timothy 5:19–20). Genuine repentance and transparent restoration processes can turn scandal into a testimony of grace and resilience (Galatians 6:1). Denominational bodies should equip victims with pastoral care and ensure that wrongdoing never evades justice, demonstrating that the church takes sin seriously (1 Corinthians 5:11). Leadership development programs that emphasize character, humility, and servant-leadership guard against pride and entitlement (Mark 10:42–45). Mentorship relationships—seasoned pastors guiding younger leaders—offer ongoing evaluation and support, reducing isolation that can lead to misconduct (Titus 1:5–9). When congregations practice church discipline lovingly and biblically, they uphold both gospel integrity and communal health (Matthew 18:15–17). These measures remind all that the church's authority derives not from office but from faithfulness to Christ's model of humble, sacrificial service (Philippians 2:5–8). In addressing failures honestly, the church can renew its mission and demonstrate the power of grace to restore even the gravest breach.

4.3 Persevering Saints—the Faithful Remnant

4.3.1 Biblical Archetypes of the Remnant

God's pattern of preserving a faithful few amid judgment emerges in the story of Noah, whose obedience in building the ark spared his family from the deluge (Genesis 7:1–5). Similarly, in Babylonian exile, Daniel and his friends refused to defile themselves, maintaining ritual and moral distinctiveness even under royal decree (Daniel 1:8; 6:10). The prophet Elijah, in despair, believed he was alone—but God revealed that 7,000 in Israel had not bowed to Baal, illustrating divine preservation of a faithful minority (1 Kings 19:18). These archetypes reveal that remnant faithfulness often requires visible dissent and steadfast reliance on God's promises (Hebrews 11:7–12). In the New Testament, Paul commends the Macedonian churches for "abounding in a wealth of generosity" despite severe trial, marking them as part of the faithful remnant (2 Corinthians 8:2). Each example teaches that perseverance in truth, even when lonely, becomes a beacon for others to rally around the genuine gospel. The remnant's faithfulness under persecution or drift serves both as a reproach to compromise and a catalyst for renewal in the larger body (James 5:17–18). By studying these precedents, modern believers gain courage to stand firm, knowing they join a heritage of saints called to uphold God's name in every generation (Revelation 12:17).

4.3.2 Marks of Genuine Fidelity

True members of the remnant display unwavering devotion to Scripture, treating it as the authoritative guide for life and doctrine (Psalm 119:105). They demonstrate integrity in speech and deed, ensuring that their "yes" means yes and their "no" means no, reflecting the character of Christ (James 1:26–27; Matthew 5:37). Compassion for the marginalized—widows, orphans, strangers—flows naturally from their love for the Lord, fulfilling Jesus' teaching that service to "the least of these" honors Him (Matthew 25:35–40). Such believers also exhibit perseverance in prayer, interceding for the church, the lost, and the nations even when answers tarry (1 Thessalonians 5:17; Romans 8:26). Their lives bear the fruit of the Spirit—love, joy, peace, patience, kindness, goodness, faithfulness, gentleness, self-control—providing tangible evidence of Christ's work within (Galatians 5:22–23). They embrace humility, acknowledging that any gifts or achievements come from God's grace rather than personal merit (Ephesians 2:8–10). True fidelity also includes a missionary impulse: they share the gospel sacrificially, knowing that faith without works is dead (James 2:14–17). Finally, they practice communal accountability, inviting correction and offering it in love, ensuring that their walk mirrors their talk (Galatians 6:1–2). These distinctives mark the faithful remnant in every context, testifying that holiness and witness are inseparable.

4.3.3 Community under Trial

In contexts where open assembly is forbidden, the remnant often meets in homes, caves, or secret locations, preserving the flame of worship against external pressure (Hebrews 10:24–25). Such house churches depend on mutual encouragement, exhorting one another daily so "none may be hardened by the deceitfulness of sin" (Hebrews 3:13). Under threat of surveillance or arrest, believers find strength in collective prayer, echoing the early Jerusalem church's devoted fellowship in Acts 4:23–31. Prophetic prayer—interceding for specific deliverance or boldness—becomes a hallmark of remnant communities, as they appeal directly to God rather than human authorities (Daniel 9:20–23). Shared hardship forges bonds of sacrificial love, with members pooling scarce resources to care for families of imprisoned or executed brethren (Acts 2:44–45). Digital tools—encrypted messaging, secure livestreams—now extend this solidarity across borders, connecting remnant cells in Asia, Africa, and the Middle East (1 Corinthians 12:12–14). Despite external hostility, these communities prioritize spiritual formation, continuing discipleship and the passing on of doctrinal truth to younger believers (2 Timothy 2:2). Their resilience under trial affirms that the church is not a building but a people shaped by suffering and hope (1 Peter 4:12–13). In witnessing to steadfast faith amid persecution, they embody the prophetic remnant called to testify until the Lamb appears (Revelation 12:11).

4.4 Historical Witnesses to Apostasy and Renewal

4.4.1 The Montanists and the Lure of Extremes

In the second century, Montanus and his followers reacted against what they perceived as a spiritually lukewarm church, claiming new prophetic revelations and an imminent New Jerusalem (cf. Revelation 21:2). While their zeal for holiness challenged complacency, their excesses—public fasting until collapse, strict asceticism, and denouncing all other ministers—revealed the danger of equating fervor with faithfulness (1 Samuel 15:22). The Montanist demand for ever-new prophecy undermined the sufficiency of Scripture, prompting Tertullian to defend a closed canon even as he sympathized with some Montanist ideals (2 Timothy 3:16–17). Their movement illustrated that zeal without doctrinal guardrails can lead to schism rather than renewal (Ephesians 4:3). Church leaders responded by affirming that any purported prophecy must align with apostolic teaching and the rule of faith (1 Corinthians 14:29; Jude 1:3). The Montanist episode thus became an early test case: genuine revival emerges not from novel visions but from deeper rooting in Christ's revealed Word (Colossians 2:6–8). Their story warns us that extremes—whether laxity or over-rigor—can obscure the gospel's center. Yet the initial impulse, a hunger for God's presence and purity, signals how the Spirit moves in times of decline to call the church back to authenticity (Revelation 2:4–5). Recognizing both error and earnestness in Montanism informs our balance of passion and fidelity today.

4.4.2 Medieval Monastic Reformers

By the tenth and eleventh centuries, monastic communities like Cluny and later the Cistercians sought to counter rampant clerical immorality and secular entanglement by returning to Benedictine simplicity (cf. Matthew 5:3–6). Cluniac reforms emphasized liturgical excellence and centralized oversight, while Cistercians under Bernard of Clairvaux championed austerity, manual labor, and contemplative prayer (Romans 12:1). These movements reinvigorated monastic spirituality, inspiring widespread reform of cathedrals and dioceses, yet they sometimes veered into elitist withdrawal from lay needs (James 2:17). Bernard's sermons on love and humility—grounded in Song of Solomon imagery—offered a corrective to legalism while guarding against mystical excess (1 John 4:16). The monastic renewals teach that structural reform without heart transformation falls short; vice versa, fervent piety without order invites chaos (1 Corinthians 14:40). They also demonstrate how communal disciplines—regular prayer offices, lectio divina, and mutual accountability—sustain holiness across generations (Hebrews 10:24–25). While medieval monasteries later faced corruption, their reformers' commitment to prayer and poverty provided a pattern for every revival phase. Their legacy reminds the church that repentance often begins in hidden places of devotion before bearing public fruit (Luke 5:16).

4.4.3 The Puritan and Pietist Revivals

Seventeenth-century Puritans in England and New England emphasized experiential faith, heart-felt assurance, and covenant renewal, responding to what they saw as a spiritually dead national church (cf. Ezekiel 36:26–27). Richard Sibbes urged believers to seek "Christ formed in you" rather than merely assent to doctrine (Galatians 4:19). Across Europe, Pietist leaders like Philipp Jakob Spener organized collegia pietatis—small groups for Bible study, accountability, and mutual care—anticipating modern cell church models (Hebrews 3:13). Their emphasis on personal conversion and sanctification stirred widespread renewal in both Lutheran and Reformed contexts, yet they sometimes faced charges of antinomianism when zeal outpaced doctrinal grounding (Galatians 5:16–18). Faithful teachers responded by coupling heartfelt devotion with robust catechesis, ensuring that experience remained tethered to truth (2 Timothy 1:13). The Puritan practice of family worship—morning and evening prayer together—embedded spiritual formation in everyday life (Deuteronomy 6:6–7). Pietist philanthropy led to orphanages and hospitals, demonstrating that true revival transforms both soul and society (Matthew 25:35–36). Through these renewals, the church learned that lasting reformation arises from movements that integrate head, heart, and hands under Scripture's authority. Their example continues to guide contemporary efforts to blend biblical fidelity with vibrant spirituality.

4.5 Spiritual Discernment—Testing the Spirits

4.5.1 Biblical Criteria for Truth

Scripture instructs us to "test the spirits to see whether they are from God," for many false prophets have gone out into the world (1 John 4:1). The primary criterion is conformity to the person and work of Christ: any spirit that denies Jesus' incarnation and atoning death is of the antichrist (1 John 4:2–3). A second test is harmony with the full counsel of God's Word: new teachings must cohere with the apostolic witness and not contradict established doctrine (Acts 20:27). Thirdly, the fruit of the Spirit—love, joy, peace, patience—serves as a living barometer of authenticity (Galatians 5:22–23); false teaching often produces discord, fear, or pride (Galatians 5:19–21). Jesus warned that wolves in sheep's clothing appear righteous but inwardly are ravenous (Matthew 7:15), reminding us that external charisma cannot substitute for inner transformation. The Bereans model noble discernment by cross-checking Paul's message against Scripture daily (Acts 17:11). Finally, communal confirmation—submission to elders and the wider church—guards against individual error (Hebrews 13:17). By applying these biblical tests, believers can navigate complex spiritual landscapes without falling prey to every novelty (2 Peter 1:3–4).

4.5.2 Cultivating a Listening Ear

Discerning God's voice amid many competing messages requires regular practices of solitude and silence, echoing Jesus' withdrawal to pray (Mark 1:35). Lectio divina—slow, prayerful reading of Scripture—invites the Spirit to illuminate God's Word for personal guidance (Psalm 119:18). Corporate discernment, exercised in prayerful gatherings, embodies the counsel of Amos: "Let justice roll down like waters, and righteousness like an ever-flowing stream" (Amos 5:24)—for justice includes truth in hearing one another under God's sovereignty. Journaling spiritual impressions helps believers track recurring themes and test them against Scripture over time (Habakkuk 2:2). Mentoring relationships and spiritual directors can provide wise feedback, helping novices distinguish emotionalism from genuine conviction (Proverbs 11:14). Fasting sharpens spiritual sensitivity by quieting bodily cravings that can distract from heavenly matters (Matthew 6:16–18). Discernment also involves community: prophetic words are to be weighed "by two or three prophets" (1 Corinthians 14:29). In this way, believers cultivate an ear attuned to the Shepherd's voice, discerning both personal callings and corporate direction.

4.5.3 Tools for Guarding the Church

Regular doctrinal reviews—through catechisms, confessions, and creeds—anchor congregations in historic, tested formulations of faith (Philippians 3:16). Bible memorization programs and structured exposition ensure that core truths permeate hearts and minds (Psalm 119:11). Pastoral councils and eldership teams provide collective oversight, reflecting Paul's model of church governance (Titus 1:5–9). External accountability, such as denominational visitations or peer review bodies, adds further checks and balances (1 Timothy 5:19–20). Spiritual formation curricula—covering theology, ethics, and spiritual disciplines—equip lay leaders to spot error in their spheres of influence (Ephesians 4:11–13). Conflict-resolution frameworks grounded in Matthew 18 help address doctrinal disputes before they fracture community (Matthew 18:15–17). Technology can aid discernment through curated theological resources, but must be used judiciously to avoid information overload (James 1:5). Prayer networks— both local and global—intercede for wisdom, echoing James' counsel that "if any of you lacks wisdom, let him ask God"

(James 1:5). These tools, wielded faithfully, guard the church against drift and foster resilience in truth.

4.6 Living as the Remnant Today

4.6.1 Holistic Obedience in an Age of Compromise

Obedience to Christ in every sphere—work, family, politics, arts—demonstrates that faith is not confined to Sunday but suffuses daily life (Colossians 3:17). In workplaces, honoring contracts and ethical standards exemplifies integrity, reflecting Christ's lordship even amid secular pressure (Romans 12:2). Within families, parents who teach children Scripture and model forgiveness embody Deuteronomy 6:6–7. Civic engagement—advocacy for the marginalized, prayer for leaders—follows Jeremiah's admonition to "seek the welfare of the city" (Jeremiah 29:7). Creative arts, when consecrated to God's glory, become worship rather than mere self-expression (Exodus 35:35). Even leisure, approached with moderation, honors God's gift of rest (Mark 6:31). By weaving obedience into every domain, the remnant displays holiness not as escapist isolation but transformative presence in the world (Matthew 5:13–16). Their lives bear witness that the gospel renews whole persons for whole communities.

4.6.2 Prophetic Courage and Compassion

Speaking truth to both church and culture requires humility, love, and a willingness to endure rejection (Ephesians 4:15). Like Nathan confronting David (2 Samuel 12:7–8), modern remnant voices must call out sin while offering paths of restoration (Galatians 6:1). Compassionate advocacy—ministering to refugees, prisoners, and the sick—grounds prophecy in mercy, recalling Jesus' compassion for the crowds (Matthew 9:36). Initiatives such as legal aid clinics or addiction recovery ministries incarnate the gospel's justice and grace (Isaiah 61:1–3). When the church refuses to compromise on core ethics yet meets needs with sacrificial love, it embodies both halves of the prophetic call—judgment and restoration (Amos 5:24). Courageous compassion attracts skeptics more than rhetoric, for it reveals the God whose love pursues the lost (Luke 15:4–7). In this dual witness, the remnant distinguishes itself from both apathetic institutions and sensationalistic movements, displaying a balanced, biblical integrity.

4.6.3 Hope-Fueled Mission amid Decline

Even as signs of drift abound, the remnant advances mission with urgency, fueled by confidence in Christ's promised return (Titus 2:13). Small cell groups and house churches multiply in contexts where large gatherings are risky, proving that size is no barrier to kingdom impact (Acts 5:42). Innovative partnerships—with NGOs, businesses, and other faith communities—leverage resources for holistic outreach without compromising gospel distinctives (1 Corinthians 9:22). Short-term mission trips and long-term cross-cultural teams bridge global and local needs, reminding the church that "the field is the world" (Matthew 13:38). Storytelling—testimonies of transformed lives—remains the church's most potent apologetic (Revelation 12:11). Digital missionaries employ social media strategically, presenting Christ to unreached audiences in culturally relevant formats (1 Corinthians 9:19–23). Through perseverance and creativity, the faithful remnant displays that decline in one area can spur innovation and deeper dependence on the Spirit (Zechariah 4:6). Their mission becomes a living prophecy that the kingdom advances even when the institutional structures wane.

Conclusion

The picture of a church splintered by error and worldliness is sobering, yet Scripture's narrative never ends in defeat. For every prophetic warning of drift, there is the testimony of faithful witnesses—ordinary believers who trusted God's Word, lived with integrity, and bore fruit in dark seasons. Their example assures us that fidelity to Christ is neither futile nor optional; it is the pathway through which God builds His eternal kingdom. As we face our own challenges—ideological pressures, moral compromises, and institutional fatigue—we are called to join this faithful remnant, reembracing the disciplines of obedience, discernment, and courageous love.

Ultimately, the drama of apostasy and survival points to a God who triumphs over every betrayal and preserves a people for His name. The same Spirit who raised up prophets, reformers, and grassroots disciples is at work today, refining the church by fire and word. May this chapter both awaken our resolve and kindle our hope, so that when Christ appears, He finds in us a people watchful, grounded, and ready to welcome our returning King.

Chapter 5. The Revelation of the Man of Lawlessness

Human history is punctuated by moments when evil appears to seize the reins of power, offering seductive promises of order, prosperity, or unity apart from God's rule. Yet Scripture unveils a climactic figure—the Man of Lawlessness—who embodies rebellion against the Creator and orchestrates a global counterfeit of Christ's kingdom. His revelation signals the nearing culmination of the age, when deception peaks and the world's systems unite under a defiant spirit. In this chapter, we will trace the portrait of this figure across Scripture, explore how he manipulates politics, economy, and religion, and discern the divine timetable that permits his rise only to bring about his swift, final overthrow. As we confront these sobering realities, our confidence rests not in human strength but in the One whose breath alone will dissolve every work of darkness.

5.1 Biblical Portraits of the Lawless One

5.1.1 Daniel's "Little Horn" and Blasphemous Power

Daniel's vision of four beasts in chapter 7 culminates in a terrifying "little horn" that arises among ten horns, speaking "magnificent things" and waging war against the saints (Daniel 7:8–25). This horn uproots three of its fellows, illustrating both its surprising origin and its ruthless ambition to dominate the ruling order. Its blasphemous speech against God ("shall wear out the saints of the Most High" and "think to change times and laws") demonstrates a direct challenge to divine authority (Daniel 7:25). The timing—"a time, times, and half a time"—connects to Old Testament prophecies of judgment and deliverance, situating the little horn within a precise prophetic timetable (Daniel 7:25). By assaulting the "Ancient of Days" and claiming equality with the Most High, this figure incarnates cosmic rebellion (Daniel 7:9–14). Yet the court convenes in heaven, and "the little horn was slain, and its body destroyed," affirming that God's justice ultimately prevails (Daniel 7:26). Daniel's interpretation shows that the little horn represents successive oppressive regimes culminating in a climactic tyrant. The vision reassures believers that—even when lawlessness seems ascendant—God's kingdom will be vindicated (Daniel 7:27). In reading Daniel, the church learns both to recognize the patterns of power and to trust the divine courtroom where the wicked are judged. Thus the "little horn" lays the foundation for understanding the Man of Lawlessness as the pinnacle of satanic defiance against God's reign.

5.1.2 Paul's "Man of Sin" in Thessalonica

In 2 Thessalonians 2:3–4, Paul warns that the Day of the Lord will not come until the "man of sin" is revealed, the one "opposing and exalting himself against every so-called god or object of worship." He calls this figure the "son of perdition," indicating destined ruin (2 Thess. 2:3). Paul speaks of "the mystery of lawlessness" already at work in the world, restrained only by a yet-undefined "one who now restrains," so that the lawless one cannot be unveiled prematurely (2 Thess. 2:7). When the restrainer is removed, this man will "take his seat in the temple of God," proclaiming himself to be God (2 Thess. 2:4), a climactic act of blasphemy. Paul stresses that this revelation will be accompanied by "all power and false signs and wonders," deceiving those who refuse love for the truth (2 Thess. 2:9–12). The apostle's pastoral concern is evident: believers must not be shaken or alarmed by these startling events (2 Thess. 2:2). He grounds their perseverance in the gospel they received, urging them to "stand firm and hold to the traditions" (2 Thess. 2:15). This passage teaches that lawlessness intensifies until a peak moment of self-deification, but that God's wrath will overtake the rebel in due time. It also underscores the importance of doctrinal clarity: knowing these truths equips the church to resist deception (2 Thess. 2:15). Paul's portrait of the man of sin thus alerts believers to the spiritual forces at work behind political and religious upheaval.

5.1.3 John's Depiction of the Beast

In Revelation 13, John sees a beast rising from the sea with ten horns and seven heads, on whose heads blasphemous names are written (Rev 13:1–2). This beast receives authority and power from the dragon, symbolizing a satanic alliance between cosmic evil and earthly power (Rev 13:2). It is granted authority to act for forty-two months, waging war on God's people and exercising authority over every tribe and nation (Rev 13:5–7). Not only does it speak proud words against the Most High, but it also wages persecution against the martyrs, displaying murderous intent (Rev 13:7). The world marvels and worships the beast, whose lethal authority extends to controlling life and death (Rev 13:4, 7). John warns of a second beast—the false prophet—who performs great signs, even calling fire down from heaven to deceive inhabitants (Rev 13:11–13). Together they enact the dragon's agenda, demanding worship of the first beast and enforcing its mark (Rev 13:12–17). The call for discernment—"Let the one who has understanding calculate the number of the beast"—underscores the need for wisdom amid deception

(Rev 13:18). Ultimately, this portrayal highlights how the Man of Lawlessness operates through political power, religious coercion, and spectacular signs. John's vision culminates in the lake of fire punishment for both beasts (Rev 19:20), reminding the church that their apparent dominion is doomed.

5.2 Mechanisms of Deception and Control

5.2.1 Political Coercion and Global Alliances

The Man of Lawlessness consolidates power through strategic alliances, forming a coalition that enforces ideological uniformity (Rev 13:7). History offers parallels in imperial cults, where subjects were compelled to offer incense to the emperor as divine lord (Acts 17:7). By demanding loyalty oaths and silencing dissent, totalitarian regimes foreshadow the beast's coercive reach (Rev 13:7). Such alliances often harness nationalist fervor, presenting the lawless one as the guarantor of security and prosperity. Through treaties and trade agreements, political leaders can legitimize authoritarian rule, marginalizing those who refuse to swear allegiance (Daniel 3:16–18). The martyrdom of those who defy compulsory worship echoes the saints slain under the beast's authority (Rev 13:7). Propaganda and state-controlled media amplify his message, drowning out contrary voices and casting resistance as treason. Yet Scripture reminds believers that "the Most High rules the kingdom of men and gives it to whom he will" (Daniel 4:17), affirming divine sovereignty even over oppressive powers. The political dimension of deception thus invites the church to pray for rulers (1 Timothy 2:1–2) and to witness courageously amid hostility. Recognizing these dynamics helps believers resist co-optation and remain faithful to Christ alone.

5.2.2 Economic Leverage and the "Mark"

Revelation 13:16–17 portrays economic control as a primary means of enforcing allegiance: "no one may buy or sell except one who has the mark." In a modern context, this typifies systems of digital currency, biometric IDs, and cashless transactions that tie economic participation to compliance. Those without the mark—refusing compromise—face deprivation and social exclusion. Historically, economic boycotts and sanctions have coerced minority populations into submission, reflecting early "no work, no eat" pressures (2 Thess. 3:10). The lure of comfort and convenience tempts many to overlook ethical costs, highlighting Jesus' warning that one cannot serve both God and money (Matthew 6:24). Yet the church is called to trust God's provision even amid scarcity, exemplified by Elijah's manna provision and Jesus feeding the five thousand (1 Kings 17:14; John 6:11). Acts of generosity—sharing resources with the needy—undermine the beast's power by demonstrating a kingdom ethics of abundance (Acts 4:34–35). Christian businesspeople can model integrity by refusing to participate in exploitative practices tied to coercive systems (Proverbs 11:1). Ultimately, the economic dimension of deception reveals how control of commerce can become an instrument of spiritual tyranny— and how the church's alternative economy of sacrificial giving proclaims a different lordship.

5.2.3 Religious Syncretism and False Worship

The Man of Lawlessness orchestrates a global religious façade, merging fragments of truth with superstition to lure the masses into unified yet hollow devotion (Rev 13:8). This syncretism recalls Old Testament apostasies, such as Israel's idol worship on high places blending Yahweh with local deities (2 Kings 17:33). The false prophet's signs and wonders— miraculous fire, healings—mimic genuine miracles, fulfilling Jesus' warning that false signs would deceive many (Matthew 24:24; 2 Thess. 2:9–10). By promising spiritual fulfillment without sacrificial obedience, such movements attract seekers weary of legalism and empty ritual. The resulting "one world religion" touts unity but lacks the cross's cost and the repentance it demands (Luke 9:23–24). Scripture calls believers to test all spirits and cling to Christ's exclusive lordship (1 John 4:1–3). Acts 17:29–31 shows how Paul confronted pagan worship by proclaiming the unknown God with clarity, a model for resisting syncretism. True worshipers must "worship in spirit and truth," honoring the Spirit's lead and the Word's authority (John 4:23–24). By rejecting counterfeit unity, the church bears witness to the only true God and to the Lamb who alone is worthy (Rev 5:12–13).

5.3 The Restrainer and the Timing of Revelation

5.3.1 Identifying the Restraining Force

Paul's reference to the one "who now restrains" lawlessness (2 Thess. 2:6–7) has sparked diverse interpretations: some identify the Holy Spirit indwelling the church, others point to the institutional church itself, and still others to civil authority. If the Spirit's convicting and sanctifying work holds back full-blown rebellion, then the church's decline coincides with escalating lawlessness. Alternatively, a stable government providing order can curb chaos, so its collapse paves the way for the son of perdition's open reign. The Bible affirms multiple agents of restraint—angelic forces dispatched to bind evil (Revelation 20:1–3), the rule of law established by God for human rulers (Romans 13:1–4), and the church's faithful witness (Matthew 16:18). Regardless of the precise identity, the gradual removal of barriers marks a divine timetable for revealing the lawless one. Believers are thus called to pray that restraint continues, even as they recognize that ultimate unveiling serves God's redemptive purpose. This interplay of sovereignty and permission reminds us that God ordains both judgment and mercy in His perfect timing (Ecclesiastes 3:1–8). Discernment of the restrainer deepens our appreciation for the Spirit's present work and our role in sustaining a counter-cultural witness.

5.3.2 The Day of Pentecost as a Foreshadowing

The outpouring of the Holy Spirit at Pentecost inaugurated a new epoch, empowering the church to preach the gospel with signs and wonders (Acts 2:1–4; 2:17–18). This Spirit-empowered witness functioned as a restraining force against satanic deception, as thousands responded to Peter's preaching rather than to false teachers. Pentecost shows how the same power that convicts the world of sin (John 16:8) also equips believers to stand firm against spiritual counterfeits. The Spirit's indwelling presence forms the true temple in which Christ reigns, countering any attempt by the lawless one to seat himself in a corrupted sanctuary. Throughout Acts, we see that persecution and false teaching notwithstanding, the gospel advances because the Spirit sustains the witness. Paul's "mystery of lawlessness" thus contrasts with the revealed mystery of godliness—Christ in us, the hope of glory (1 Timothy 3:16). Pentecost's pattern reminds the remnant that the Spirit's gifting and fruit are foundational to discerning and defeating lawlessness. By renewing reliance on Spirit baptism and charisms, the church reactivates the restraining power in its midst.

5.3.3 Signs Preceding His Unveiling

Scripture indicates that broad apostasy is a precursor to the lawless one's revelation: "unless the apostasy comes first…he will be revealed" (2 Thess. 2:3). We see this in diminishing commitment to Christ's lordship, as many profess faith yet live as if He were absent (Matthew 7:21–23). Spiritual warfare intensifies alongside moral decay, as demonic forces find greater footholds when the church's prayerful intercession wanes (Ephesians 6:12–18). Cosmic disturbances—earthquakes, famines, plagues—often accompany signposts of both judgment and mercy (Luke 21:25–28). These birth-pangs signal that the day of the Lord draws near, and that the man of lawlessness's hour approaches amid increasing chaos. Yet each sign also invites repentance, for God's desire is that none should perish (2 Peter 3:9). Jesus linked global tribulations with the fig-tree parable, urging discernment and readiness (Matthew 24:32–33). Believers thus track both external upheavals and internal spiritual health, recognizing that true readiness lies in holiness rather than headline watching. As apostasy peaks, the remnant clings all the more tightly to God's unchanging promises, confident that every dark sign precedes divine dawn.

5.4 Confrontation and Overthrow

5.4.1 Christ's "Breath of His Mouth" Victory

When the Man of Lawlessness reaches the apex of his power, Scripture reveals that his undoing comes not by human force but by the sovereign word of Christ: "the Lord Jesus will kill him with the breath of his mouth" (2 Thessalonians 2:8). This image evokes Isaiah's prophecy that the sovereign Lord "will strike the earth with the rod of his mouth, and with the breath of his lips he will kill the wicked" (Isaiah 11:4). The "breath" signifies the authoritative word, underscoring that divine decree alone can dismantle the kingdom of rebellion. No human army or political coalition can match the power of Christ's spoken command. In John's vision, the Word of God is personified as a sharp two-edged sword coming from Christ's mouth (Revelation 1:16), emphasizing that truth and judgment issue together. This decisive act affirms God's ultimate sovereignty over every counterfeit throne and idol (Psalm 2:4–6). The abruptness of the breath—swift and unerring—illustrates that lawlessness, however entrenched, cannot stand against divine opposition. Believers can therefore face the reign of the man of lawlessness without fear, knowing that Christ's victory is certain and imminent. As Paul exhorts, "Be steadfast, immovable, always abounding in the work of the Lord" (1 Corinthians 15:58), for the very moment we endure brings us closer to his triumphant return. This portrayal encourages the church to trust in Christ's word above all earthly powers.

5.4.2 The Defeat of the Beast and False Prophet

Following Christ's swift overthrow of the lawless one, Revelation recounts the binding of Satan and the doom of his accomplices: "the beast was captured, and with it the false prophet who in its presence had done the signs" (Revelation 19:20). The imagery of two figures cast alive into the lake of fire underscores the personal responsibility of both political and religious deceivers. The false prophet's ability to perform miraculous signs—calling down fire (Revelation 13:13) and deceiving the masses—symbolizes the seductive power of counterfeit spirituality. Their joint fate illustrates that no spiritual or temporal alliance can withstand divine justice. Binding the dragon (Satan) for a thousand years (Revelation 20:1–3) further removes the source of weekly rebellion, inaugurating a period of peace under Christ's rule. This chronological separation between the defeat of the beast and the binding of Satan highlights God's meticulous control of history. The final act of casting into the lake of fire (Revelation 20:10) brings cosmic closure to the drama of evil. These judgments reassure the remnant that endurance through persecution will be vindicated. They also signal to the world that true authority belongs to God alone, not to transient powers. Ultimately, this section calls the church to await with hope the final eradication of every foe.

5.4.3 Vindication of the Saints

The downfall of the Man of Lawlessness sets the stage for the vindication and vindictive reward of God's faithful: "the souls of those who had been beheaded for the testimony of Jesus and for the word of God…came to life and reigned with Christ for a thousand years" (Revelation 20:4–6). This passage affirms that martyrdom is not in vain but leads to resurrection life and shared reign with Christ. The "first resurrection" marks the honored status of those who remained loyal, contrasting with the spiritual death of the wicked (Revelation 20:5). Their reward echoes Paul's words, "If we endure, we will also reign with him" (2 Timothy 2:12). This reign is both present—in the communion of the saints—and future, in the restored new creation. The prophetic assurance of reigning with Christ inspires believers to persevere amid trials, knowing that suffering now leads to glory then (Romans 8:18). Revelation's vision of worship around the throne (Revelation 4–5) further underscores that vindication culminates in unbroken fellowship with the Lamb. The saints' reign also functions as a testimony to the world of God's faithfulness and justice. Their restored sovereignty over creation reflects God's original mandate to humanity (Genesis 1:28), now fully realized. In this way, the church's suffering history is woven into the triumphant future of the kingdom.

5.5 Theological Implications of the Lawless One

5.5.1 God's Sovereignty over Evil

The emergence and defeat of the Man of Lawlessness highlight a paradox: God permits a period of unprecedented rebellion, yet He remains sovereign throughout. Paul affirms that the lawless one is allowed to operate "in accordance with the activity of Satan" (2 Thessalonians 2:9), yet even Satan and his agents serve under divine permission (Job 1:12; Luke 22:31–32). This "permissive will" underscores that God's judgments often include allowing evil to run its course before executing final justice (Romans 9:17). At the same time, Scripture insists that God's wrath is revealed against all ungodliness (Romans 1:18), ensuring that evil never escapes accountability. The theological tension between permissiveness and sovereignty teaches believers to trust that present chaos fits into God's redemptive plan (Isaiah 55:8–9). It also affirms that no power can thwart the unfolding of His purposes (Job 42:2; Daniel 4:35). The reality of divine control provides comfort to the faithful remnant: suffering is neither random nor unobserved (Psalm 56:8). It encourages a posture of humble submission, acknowledging the mystery of God's governance (Deuteronomy 29:29). Ultimately, the sovereignty theme directs worship heavenward, for "worthy is the Lamb who was slain" to receive authority and praise (Revelation 5:12).

5.5.2 Eschatological Ethics in the Face of Deception

Knowing that the Man of Lawlessness will use deception, coercion, and counterfeit signs to subvert truth, Christians are called to live eschatological ethics—values shaped by future hope. Paul exhorts believers: "Do not be conformed to this world, but be transformed by the renewal of your mind" (Romans 12:2). This transformation manifests in courageous truth-telling, sacrificial love, and refusal to participate in systems that betray Christ's lordship. Ethical decision-making must anticipate Christ's return, choosing obedience even at personal cost (Matthew 10:28). Jesus' call to be "wise as serpents and innocent as doves" (Matthew 10:16) applies acutely when false prophets abound. The church's countercultural moral witness—hospitality to refugees, care for the poor, defense of justice—demonstrates the kingdom in action (Micah 6:8). In business and technology, refusing to acquiesce to coercive economic measures honors God above profit (Matthew 6:24). In public life, prophetic speech that challenges injustice reflects Daniel's courage in exile (Daniel 6). Such ethics not only resist deception but also point to the integrity of the coming kingdom. They remind the world that ultimate allegiance belongs to the risen Lord, not to any temporal authority.

5.5.3 Hope and Comfort for Persecuted Believers

The account of the Man of Lawlessness offers profound comfort to those suffering for Christ's name. Jesus promised, "In the world you will have tribulation. But take heart; I have overcome the world" (John 16:33). This victory narrative assures believers that persecution is not the final word but a prelude to resurrection and reign (Revelation 2:10; 20:4–6). Hebrews encourages, "Remember your leaders...consider the outcome of their way of life, and imitate their faith" (Hebrews 13:7), pointing to martyrs who now share in triumph. The promise of Christ's presence—"I am with you always" (Matthew 28:20)—sustains endurance amid the onslaught of the beast's regime. Revelation depicts the martyrs under the altar crying, "How long...?" until given white robes, symbolizing vindication (Revelation 6:9–11). This imagery assures that God hears every cry and will respond in his timing. Persecuted communities can cling to James' exhortation to "count it all joy...when you meet trials" (James 1:2–4), knowing trials refine faith. The hope of sharing Christ's glory fuels witness: "If we suffer with him, we will also reign with him" (2 Timothy 2:12). Thus, the remnant stands under trial with courage, sustained by the certainty that faithfulness leads to eternal reward.

5.6 Practical Readiness for the Remnant

5.6.1 Discernment through Scripture and Spirit

To recognize the Man of Lawlessness amid deception, the church must ground its discernment both in the written Word and in the illuminating work of the Spirit. John instructs, "By this you know the Spirit of God...every spirit that confesses that Jesus Christ has come in the flesh is from God" (1 John 4:2–3). Consistent, communal Bible study in churches and small groups equips believers to identify teachings that contradict apostolic doctrine (Acts 17:11). Regular immersion in Scripture transforms the mind and forms a "plumb line" of truth against which all messages are measured (Isaiah 28:17). Simultaneously, prayerful dependence on the Spirit—seeking His guidance in corporate gatherings and personal devotion— enables immediate testing of emerging teachings (John 16:13). Fast-paced, media-driven culture can dull spiritual sensitivity; spiritual disciplines such as silence, solitude, and fasting sharpen perceptiveness (Matthew 6:16–18). Mentorship and discipleship relationships provide additional layers of accountability, ensuring personal impressions align with biblical truth (Proverbs 11:14). Technology can aid discernment through trusted theological resources, but must be used judiciously to avoid information overload (James 1:5). Through these combined means, the remnant stands prepared, neither naïve nor cynical, but anchored in Word and Spirit.

5.6.2 Community Formation under Persecution

As the Man of Lawlessness intensifies persecution, the faithful remnant must cultivate resilient, redemptive communities. The early church "devoted themselves to the apostles' teaching and to fellowship...in homes" (Acts 2:42–46), modeling how scattered believers can sustain one another. House churches and cell networks provide safe venues for worship, mutual encouragement, and practical aid when official structures collapse. Shared economic resources and hospitality extend the church's witness to neighbors and strengthen internal solidarity (Romans 12:13). Digital platforms—encrypted messaging, secure livestreams—now facilitate cross-border fellowship, prayer, and discipleship in regions hostile to the gospel (1 Corinthians 12:12–14). Training of lay elders and deacons ensures leadership continuity when persecution decapitates formal hierarchies (Titus 1:5–9). Regular times of corporate fasting, intercession, and Scripture reading empower communities to stand firm (Joel 2:12–13). Storytelling—sharing testimonies of God's faithfulness under pressure—fosters hope and identity (Revelation 12:11). These resilient networks thus embody Christ's body on earth, reflecting his promise that "where two or three are gathered...he is there in the midst of them" (Matthew 18:20).

5.6.3 Proclaiming Christ as True King

Ultimately, the church's antidote to lawlessness is bold proclamation of Christ's exclusive lordship. Peter and John declared, "We must obey God rather than men" (Acts 5:29), exemplifying courage before sinful authorities. Evangelistic efforts in defiant contexts—street preaching, digital outreach, relational witness—announce that Jesus alone is King (Philippians 2:9–11). Musical, artistic, and literary expressions provide culturally adaptable vehicles for proclaiming the gospel under oppressive regimes. Street pastors, marketplace believers, and student groups function as prophetic outposts, embodying the reign of Christ in everyday spheres (Matthew 5:14–16). Strategic use of covert literature distribution— smuggled Bibles, audio Scriptures—perpetuates the faithful witness when open assemblies are banned (Psalm 119:46). Public acts of mercy—feeding the hungry, visiting prisoners— demonstrate Christ's compassion and challenge the beast's cold calculation (Matthew 25:35–40). As the remnant proclaims the Lamb's worthiness, they call all people to renounce allegiance to every counterfeit king. This witness, rooted in Scripture and empowered by the Spirit, anticipates the day when "every tongue will confess that Jesus Christ is Lord" before God the Father (Philippians 2:11).

Conclusion

Confronting the reality of the Man of Lawlessness sharpens the church's urgency to stand firm in truth and to embody the light of Christ amid encroaching shadows. While his deception will captivate many, the same Scriptures that warn us of his tactics also reveal the unassailable victory of our Lord—who alone carries the authority to judge and to save. In understanding the contours of this final rebellion, believers gain not dread but determination: to walk in holiness, to test every spirit, and to proclaim boldly that Jesus is King over every throne. May this knowledge inspire a vigilant and courageous remnant, ever ready to witness to the living Christ until the very moment He renders lawlessness powerless and ushers in the everlasting reign of righteousness.

Chapter 6. Tribulation, Judgment, and Divine Mercy

The unfolding drama of the end times reveals a God who neither shrinks from judging entrenched evil nor withholds compassion from a repentant world. In the passages that chart the seals, trumpets, and bowls, we witness the cosmic courtroom in session, where every rebellion is exposed and every plea for mercy is heard. These visions remind us that tribulation is neither arbitrary nor gratuitous, but serves to unmask the depth of human sin, call the lost to repentance, and purify the faithful remnant. As we explore this sobering yet hopeful panorama, we will discover that even in the darkest outpouring of wrath, God's lovingkindness shines through—sealing His people, sending His messengers with final invitations, and sustaining our endurance by the promise of ultimate redemption.

6.1 The Seven Seals: Opening Heaven's Court

6.1.1 The First Seal—Conquering White Horse

The first seal reveals a rider on a white horse, carrying a bow and given a crown, who goes out "conquering and to conquer" (Revelation 6:2). On the surface, this image echoes Christ's victorious return, yet its context within the seals suggests a deceptive counterpart—a counterfeit messianic figure. The crown he receives (Greek: *stephanos*) implies a fleeting victory rather than the eternal reign promised to Christ (Revelation 19:12). The bow, without arrows, may symbolize threats or intimidation rather than genuine provision of peace. Historically, oppressive rulers have claimed divine sanction to unify nations under the guise of peace, echoing this antichristic parody. Yet the church's witness to the true Gospel advances even amid such false triumphs, as Christ's kingdom grows invisibly through Spirit-empowered proclamation (Matthew 24:14). Believers are called to discern genuine spiritual conquest—lives transformed by the cross—from the seductive but empty victories of authoritarian regimes. Early Christians understood that white garments and crowns in Scripture signify righteousness and reward (Revelation 3:5; 2 Timothy 4:8), not coercive conquest. Thus this first seal both warns of a powerful deception and reminds the remnant to cling to the true victor, whose arrows are words of justice and grace (Ephesians 6:17). The counter-Gospel of the white horse demands sober vigilance and unwavering allegiance to Christ alone.

6.1.2 The Second Seal—War on Earth

The opening of the second seal summons forth a rider on a red horse, granted power to take peace from the earth and incite people to slaughter one another (Revelation 6:3–4). This red horse vividly portrays escalating global conflict—civil wars, political uprisings, and ethnic strife—that foreshadow deeper spiritual warfare. Jesus warned His disciples that they would witness "wars and rumors of wars" before His return (Matthew 24:6), and the imagery here intensifies that warning into divine judgment upon humanity's bloodlust. The removal of peace contrasts starkly with the Prince of Peace, who bore human hostility yet offers reconciliation through the cross (Colossians 1:20). Historically, world wars and genocides have demonstrated mankind's capacity to weaponize technology and ideology for destruction on an unprecedented scale. Yet the church's mission—to proclaim the gospel of peace—shines brightest amid such darkness (Ephesians 6:15). Believers are therefore called to intercede for peace (Psalm 122:6), to work for reconciliation in their spheres (2 Corinthians 5:18–19), and to remind the world that true peace comes only through Christ's sacrificial love. The red horse also signals that political solutions alone cannot end the cycle of violence; only divine intervention can heal the nations (Isaiah 2:4). By naming the spiritual roots of conflict—sin, pride, and rebellion—followers of Jesus bear witness to the deeper peace of God (Philippians 4:7). In this way, the second seal both judges human warfare and galvanizes the church's peacemaking witness.

6.1.3 The Third and Fourth Seals—Famine and Death

The third seal unveils a rider on a black horse holding scales, and a voice declares the scarcity of basic foodstuffs—wheat, barley, oil, and wine—signifying famine and economic collapse (Revelation 6:5–6). The scales evoke careful measurement, suggesting rationing and inequality in distribution, often prevalent in times of crisis. Jesus taught that "man shall not live by bread alone" (Luke 4:4), yet famine exposes how deeply societies depend on material provision. The black horse's color—symbolic of mourning—reflects the spiritual and physical deprivation brought by broken systems. The fourth seal introduces a pale horse named Death, whose rider is Hades, granted authority over a quarter of the earth to kill by sword, famine, pestilence, and wild beasts (Revelation 6:7–8). This multifaceted death mirrors the four horsemen's cumulative devastation, reminding us that judgment is both diverse and comprehensive. The inclusion of pestilence and wild beasts evokes Old Testament plagues, illustrating that divine judgment often comes through nature turned against humanity (Exodus 9:3; Amos 5:19). Yet Scripture also promises that God "will be merciful to the remnant" when famine and pestilence strike (Zechariah 8:12). The church's response in such times includes hanging onto the promise that "by His stripes we are healed" (Isaiah 53:5) and caring for the afflicted as an expression of the gospel (Matthew 25:35–36). Through these seals, the divine court unveils humanity's brokenness and calls the faithful remnant to unwavering trust in God's sustaining grace, even amid scarcity and death.

6.2 The Trumpets: Warnings and Calls to Repentance

6.2.1 Trumpets One–Four: Nature's Rebuke

As the seventh seal introduces seven trumpets, the first four trumpets unleash ecological judgments upon earth, sea, rivers, and skies (Revelation 8:7–12). Hail and fire mixed with blood burn a third of the trees and grass, representing divine indignation that consumes human pride and threatens natural order (Rev 8:7). A mountain ablaze thrown into the sea turns a third of it to blood, killing marine life and laying bare the interconnectedness of creation (Rev 8:8–9). Rivers and springs turning bitter recall Moses' miracle at Marah, where God transformed bitterness into healing, contrasting divine mercy with unleashed wrath (Exodus 15:23–26; Rev 8:10–11). The darkening of a third of sun, moon, and stars signals cosmic sorrow—creation itself mourning the moral rebellion of its stewards (Rev 8:12). Joel's prophecy that the sun will be turned to darkness before the Day of the Lord underscores these trumpet judgments as preludes to final reckoning (Joel 2:31). Earth's rebuke functions as a call to repentance, for natural calamities often awaken hearts to divine sovereignty (Psalm 46:6–8). The call to heed these warnings echoes Jesus' parable urging readiness, for such signs signal the nearness of redemption (Luke 21:28). The remnant responds by interceding for the world, proclaiming that repentance averts deeper judgments (2 Chronicles 7:14). In this way, trumpets one through four both pronounce judgment and offer a window of mercy through genuine contrition.

6.2.2 The Fifth Trumpet—The Scorpion Locusts

The fifth trumpet opens the bottomless pit, releasing demonic locusts given power like scorpions to torment those without the seal of God (Revelation 9:1–2, 3–6). Unlike agricultural locusts that destroy vegetation, these beings afflict human flesh with stinging torment, symbolizing spiritual affliction and demonic influence. Their instruction "not to harm the grass or any green thing…only those people who do not have the seal of God" (Rev 9:4) highlights divine protection for the faithful, even in judgment. The scorpion-locusts' ability to torment for five months parallels the limited mercy God extends before final doom (Rev 9:5; Exodus 10:4). This terrifying image reminds believers that spiritual warfare intensifies as rebellion deepens, and that only God's seal—His ownership—offers safety. Yet even this grim visitation carries a merciful aim: to drive hardened hearts to seek relief and find refuge in Christ (Luke 13:24–27). The duration of torment underscores the disciplined nature of God's judgments, not random cruelty (Rev 9:5). Early church fathers interpreted these scourges as both literal and symbolic, urging the church to endure through faith (Eph 6:12). Contemporary readers see in global crises— pandemics, ideological addictions—a parallel spiritual suffering calling for repentance. The five months of torment thus function as an extended invitation to trust God's deliverance, lest the deeper plagues follow.

6.2.3 The Sixth Trumpet—Four Angels Released

The sixth trumpet unleashes four angels bound at the great river Euphrates, releasing an army of 200 million horsemen to kill a third of mankind (Revelation 9:13–15). The Euphrates, a historic boundary in Israel's narrative, here becomes a launching point for divine judgment, evoking Old Testament humiliations of Israel's enemies (Jeremiah 51:33–36). The massive scale of this army—symbolic of overwhelming force—reflects the breadth of rebellion and the seriousness with which God addresses collective sin (Rev 9:16). The mention of horsemen with breastplates the color of fire, hyacinth, and sulfur highlights the fusion of natural and supernatural elements in these judgments. This vision underscores that divine justice employs human instruments—historical armies and political powers—within God's sovereign plan (Isaiah 10:5–19). Yet the remnant, sealed by God, is exempt from this slaughter, illustrating that God's discipline distinguishes between His own and the unrepentant (Rev 7:3–4). The army's command to kill by fire, smoke, and sulfur points to catastrophic, multi-dimensional judgment (Rev 9:18). As in Daniel's visions of fiery beasts, such terrors proclaim God's holiness and mankind's culpability (Daniel 7:9–11). The sixth trumpet stands as a sobering reminder that the stakes of spiritual allegiance are cosmic in scope. Believers are therefore urged to persevere in faith, knowing that God's protective seal secures them through every upheaval.

6.3 The Bowls of Wrath: Final Outpouring

6.3.1 Bowls One–Four: Intensifying Torment

The first four bowls pour out intensified judgments—sores on those bearing the beast's mark, the sea and rivers turned to blood, the sun scorching people, and darkness upon the beast's throne (Revelation 16:2–10). The painful sores echo the plagues of Egypt, signifying that stubborn refusal to repent brings physical suffering (Exodus 9:9–11). Water turned to blood recalls both Noah's flood and the first Egyptian plague, symbolizing that all life is sacred yet susceptible to divine wrath (Genesis 9:4–5; Exodus 7:19–21). The scorching sun intensifies human misery, yet those afflicted still refuse to glorify God or repent (Rev 16:9), illustrating human hardness of heart. The darkness over the beast's kingdom underscores that even satanic dominion cannot withstand God's condemnation (Rev 16:10). Each bowl escalates the severity of judgment, moving from individual affliction to ecological and cosmic disturbance. Yet Scripture states that these plagues are "true and righteous" because they arise from the blood of saints and apostles shed by persecutors (Rev 16:5–6). This divine justice corrects historical wrongs and vindicates the church's witness. The remnant finds comfort that God remembers their sufferings and issues perfect retribution. In this way, bowls one through four reveal the depth of divine holiness and the inevitability of judgment when mercy is spurned.

6.3.2 The Fifth Bowl—Kingdom Darkness

The fifth bowl plunges the beast's kingdom into utter darkness, causing people to gnaw their tongues in agony yet refusing repentance (Revelation 16:10–11). This darkness evokes the plague of darkness in Egypt but surpasses it in spiritual significance, as even the beast's throne is enshrouded (Exodus 10:21–23). The psychological terror of impenetrable gloom emphasizes humanity's plight when separated from the light of God's presence (John 8:12). Yet this very experience calls to mind Jesus' promise to be the light in our darkness (John 1:4–5). The refusal to repent despite intense suffering illustrates the hardness of sinful hearts under judgment (Jeremiah 5:3). The five "wounds" inflicted upon the beast's followers mirror those the beast delivered to the church earlier (Rev 13:3–4), completing a cycle of retribution. This bowl also symbolically enacts prophetic warnings that the wicked will "walk in darkness with no light" (Isaiah 8:22). The remnant, sealed by God, remains in the light of His Word and Spirit (Isaiah 42:6). By contrasting divine light with demonic darkness, this judgment reaffirms that true life and guidance flow only from Christ. Believers are therefore called to hold fast to the light of Christ, even when the world is engulfed in the beast's shadow.

6.3.3 The Sixth and Seventh Bowls—Battle Preparations and Cataclysm

The sixth bowl dries up the Euphrates to prepare the way for the kings of the east, and unclean spirits gather the world for the battle of Armageddon (Revelation 16:12–16). The drying of the Euphrates, a life-giving river, signals that human efforts to circumvent God's sovereignty will instead pave the way for ultimate judgment. The gathering at Armageddon—a symbolic mountain of Megiddo—evokes Israel's storied battlefields where God's deliverance was most evident (Judges 4–5). This convergence of demonic forces heralds the climactic showdown between good and evil, yet it also underscores that the outcome is already determined by divine decree (Revelation 17:14). The seventh bowl brings a tremendous earthquake and hailstones weighing about a talent each, collapsing islands and mountains (Revelation 16:17–20). The global scale of this cataclysm mirrors the plagues of Genesis and Exodus, completing the cycle of creation's rebellion and redemption (Genesis 1; Ex. 19:18). Every topographical and social structure is leveled, reminding the world that no human institution can withstand divine power. In the aftermath, a voice proclaims, "It is done!" (Rev 16:17), echoing Christ's cry of completion on the cross (John 19:30). This final bowl ushers in the defeat of the beast and the false prophet (Rev 19:20) and sets the stage for God's kingdom to come in fullness. The remnant emerges from these judgments as the seedbed for the renewed creation, purified and prepared for eternal fellowship with God.

6.4 The Purpose of Divine Judgment

6.4.1 Vindication of God's Holiness

Divine judgment displays the essential purity and justice of God's character, confronting every form of rebellion and corruption. When a righteous God judges sin, He affirms that evil is neither trivial nor harmless but deeply offensive to His holy nature (Psalm 89:14). The plagues and persecutions described in the seals, trumpets, and bowls make visible what is hidden: the extent to which human pride and violence degrade God's good creation. By executing judgment, God demonstrates that He is not indifferent to suffering; rather, He acts decisively to correct and to restore justice (Isaiah 61:8). These actions vindicate His name before the universe, showing that His ways are true and right (Deuteronomy 32:4). Judgment also serves to uphold the honor of those who remain faithful: when wicked systems collapse under divine wrath, the integrity of the oppressed is publicly affirmed (Psalm 96:10). In this way, God's holiness becomes a sanctuary and a shield for the remnant, reminding them that He will not allow His name to be profaned indefinitely (Ezekiel 36:23). Furthermore, judgment against evil reassures believers that suffering and injustice are not permanent; God will right every wrong in His timing (Romans 12:19). Thus, the purpose of judgment is not vindictive cruelty but the restoration of cosmic harmony and the vindication of the faithful.

6.4.2 Warning to Unrepentant Humanity

The unfolding judgments serve as both proclamation and warning: before the final bowl falls, God gives humanity every opportunity to turn from sin. Scripture depicts God's patience as a crucial aspect of His character: "He is patient toward you, not wishing that any should perish, but that all should reach repentance" (2 Peter 3:9). Each plague, earthquake, or famine functions like a prophetic alarm bell, urging people to heed the voice of the covenant: "If anyone hears my voice and does not harden his heart" (Hebrews 3:15). The trumpet and bowl judgments intensify in sequence, reflecting escalating divine appeals—from mild warning to severe rebuke—before the final, irreversible sentence. Yet even amid terror, the message remains consistent: repentance and faith in Christ offer deliverance (Joel 2:12–13). The contrast between those who bear the seal of God and those who succumb to judgment highlights the choice presented to every individual (Revelation 7:3). Historical examples—from Nineveh's temporary revival under Jonah's preaching to the remnant restored after exile—demonstrate that genuine turning to God can avert deeper calamity (Jonah 3:5–10; Isaiah 44:22). Thus, judgment is not arbitrary but redemptive in purpose, driven by a God who desires relationship over retribution (Ezekiel 18:23). For the unrepentant, these warnings fall on deaf ears, but for the open-hearted, they become God's merciful wake–up call.

6.4.3 Purification of a Faithful Remnant

Through trials and judgments, God refines His people like gold tested by fire, removing dross and deepening their faith (1 Peter 1:6–7). The imagery of refining fire underscores that suffering—even when intense—is used by God to remove unbelief, worldliness, and compromise. As Isaiah observed, "For when your judgments are in the earth, the people of the world learn righteousness" (Isaiah 26:9); the remnant emerges from tribulation with a purer devotion to Christ. This process of purification fosters unity among believers, since shared trials cultivate mutual compassion, humility, and dependence on the Spirit (Hebrews 12:10–11). The sealing of the 144,000 (Rev 7:3–4) protects the faithful remnant from the worst of the wrath, marking them as God's own. This seal symbolizes not only safety but also ownership: the remnant belongs wholly to the Lord, set apart for His purposes amid global upheaval. As suffering empties lives of self–reliance, the remnant learns to trust God alone, fulfilling Jesus' promise that "whoever loses his life for my sake will save it" (Luke 9:24). Their endurance bears witness to the world that God's power is made perfect in weakness (2 Corinthians 12:9). Through purification, the remnant becomes the living temple of God, ready to display His glory in the renewed creation (Revelation 21:3–4).

6.5 Divine Mercy Amid Wrath

6.5.1 The 144,000 Sealed Servants

Before the trumpet judgments unfold, John sees 144,000 servants of God sealed on their foreheads for protection (Revelation 7:3–4). These servants—12,000 from each tribe of Israel—represent a purified, covenantal fidelity that transcends ethnic and religious boundaries. Their sealing echoes Ezekiel's vision of the mark on righteous remnant (Ezekiel 9:4), signifying divine ownership and security amid judgment. This seal is not a magical talisman but a covenant marker, indicating that God's judgment passes over those under His banner (Exodus 12:7, 13). The number 144,000 signifies completeness: 12 (tribes) × 12 (apostolic foundation) × 1,000 (plentitude). Their witness in the midst of tribulation exemplifies how God builds His church through faithful minority rather than overwhelming majority (Matthew 16:18). The sealed remnant contrasts starkly with those marked by the beast, underscoring the cosmic choice between allegiance to God and to antichristic powers. As they sing the song of Moses and the Lamb (Rev 15:3), their role foreshadows the global harvest that follows when souls from every nation join their ranks (Rev 7:9). Their preservation reveals God's mercy at work even while wrath unfolds, showing that He both disciplines and delivers His own.

6.5.2 Angelic Declarations of the Everlasting Gospel

Interspersed among the judgments, three angels proclaim the "everlasting gospel" to every tribe, language, people, and nation (Revelation 14:6–7). The first angel's call, "Fear God and give him glory, for the hour of his judgment has come," links gospel proclamation with the urgency of impending reckoning. This angelic message underscores divine mercy: even as wrath falls, God offers the good news of forgiveness and peace through Christ (Romans 5:1–2). The second angel pronounces Babylon's fall, warning against spiritual adulteries that betray the bridegroom (Rev 14:8). The third angel cautions against worshiping the beast or receiving his mark, for "the wrath of God" follows upon the unrepentant (Rev 14:9–11). These declarations function as final trumpets of mercy, giving all a last opportunity to align with God's kingdom. Their global reach recalls the Great Commission's mandate, showing that angelic proclamation complements human evangelism in mission (Matthew 28:19–20). By juxtaposing gospel calls with judgment announcements, Scripture emphasizes that true mercy often comes on the eve of justice, compelling decisive response. In this way, divine mercy shines brightest amid divine wrath, extending grace to whosoever will (Revelation 22:17).

6.5.3 Intercession of the Martyrs

Beneath the altar in heaven, John sees the souls of martyrs who had been slain for the word of God, crying out, "How long...until you avenge our blood?" (Revelation 6:9–10). Their cry illustrates that even in heaven, believers bear witness to injustice and intercede for righteous judgment. God responds by giving them white robes and telling them to rest until their number is complete, indicating a measured divine timetable for vindication (Rev 6:11). This intercession reveals that martyrdom is not a silent sacrifice but an active plea in God's court, contributing to the outworking of His justice. Hebrews affirms that "the blood of martyrs" speaks more loudly than any coercive power, penetrating the gates of heaven with righteous demand (Hebrews 11:35–38). The martyrs' role also comforts the living remnant: they are not forgotten, and their suffering helps usher in the kingdom (Luke 16:25–26). Their intercession underscores the solidarity between the church militant on earth and the church triumphant in heaven. As the bowls and trumpets advance, the martyrs' cry fuels God's timing, ensuring that wrath and mercy unfold in perfect balance. Ultimately, their witness confirms that God hears every act of faithfulness, weaving martyrdom into the tapestry of redemption (Revelation 7:13–17).

6.6 Living Through Tribulation

6.6.1 Endurance and Overcoming Faith

Jesus warned His followers that "in this world you will have tribulation" but promised that "he who endures to the end shall be saved" (John 16:33; Matthew 24:13). Endurance is not mere stubbornness but active perseverance rooted in a relationship with Christ. Spiritual disciplines—prayer, Scripture meditation, fasting—sustain believers when external pressures mount (1 Thessalonians 5:17; Psalm 119:105). The epistles exhort the church to rejoice in suffering, knowing that trials produce steadfastness and mature character (James 1:2–4; Romans 5:3–5). Overcoming faith emerges as believers choose obedience over comfort, trusting God's promises amid uncertainty (Hebrews 11:1). Community stories of perseverance—Acts of faith under persecution—encourage others to stand firm (Acts 14:22). The remnant's resilience testifies that tribulation is not the cessation of God's blessing but a refining fire that draws hidden resources of grace to the surface. As the author of Hebrews reminds, "let us run with endurance the race that is set before us, looking to Jesus" (Hebrews 12:1–2). In this way, tribulation becomes a dynamic training ground for victorious faith.

6.2 Corporate Solidarity and Prayer

In times of trial, the early church "devoted themselves to the apostles' teaching and to fellowship, to the breaking of bread and to prayer" (Acts 2:42). Shared worship and prayer conferences—like the seven days of worship in Revelation 8:1–5—sustain collective hope. Corporate fasting and intercession activate God's promises of refuge and strength (Isaiah 58:6–12). Small groups and house churches become lifelines, providing practical aid, emotional support, and theological grounding (Hebrews 10:24–25). Intercessory prayer for persecuted brothers and sisters fosters global solidarity, reminding the remnant that they are part of a worldwide body (1 Corinthians 12:26). The "song of Moses and the Lamb" sung by the martyrs (Rev 15:3) becomes the communal hymn of overcoming, transcending cultural and linguistic divides. Communal prayer also functions as a witness to unbelievers, demonstrating the power of God to unite diverse believers in adversity (John 17:20–23). In every season of tribulation, the church's corporate solidarity and prayer underscore that victory over darkness is shared, not solo.

6.3 Hope in the Promise of Redemption

Amid tribulation, the remnant's ultimate anchor is the vision of the New Heavens and New Earth, where God "will dwell with His people" and "death shall be no more" (Revelation 21:3–4). This future hope transforms present suffering into anticipation, for every trial now is but a "light and momentary affliction" compared to the "eternal weight of glory" (2 Corinthians 4:17).

The promise of a renewed creation restores the original mandate to "fill the earth and subdue it" under Christ's benevolent rule (Genesis 1:28; Revelation 22:3). Frequent remembrance of this hope—through liturgy, art, and personal meditation—guards believers against despair and nihilism (Romans 15:13). Early Christians etched the fish symbol and the chi–rho on catacomb walls to proclaim their confidence in ultimate resurrection and renewal. Modern worship songs and hymns that focus on the heavenly city continue this tradition, directing hearts away from temporal worries toward eternal realities. Theological reflection on redemption history—from creation's groaning (Romans 8:22–23) to consummation—strengthens resolve to live faithfully now. Thus, hope in redemption is not escapism but the power that sustains the remnant through every judgment, until the God of mercies makes all things new.

Conclusion

Though the earth convulses and the heavens pour out judgment, the true story is one of restoration and mercy triumphing over despair. Every moment of trial is infused with a divine purpose: to refine our faith, awaken repentant hearts, and prepare the way for a new creation where sorrow and death are banished forever. For those who stand firm, these chapters offer both warning and assurance—that in the very presence of God's righteous fury we find the shelter of His covenant love. May this vision galvanize us to live lives of courageous hope, confident that the same hand that brings judgment will in the end wipe away every tear and welcome us into the joy of His everlasting peace.

Chapter 7. Israel and the Ingathering of the Nations

From the dawn of redemptive history, God's heart has been set on gathering a people for Himself from every tribe and tongue. He began with a promise to Abraham, advanced through the law and the prophets, and was inaugurated in Christ's first advent—yet the story is far from complete. Centuries of exile, return, and scattering have borne witness to both human failure and divine faithfulness, reminding us that physical borders cannot contain His saving purpose. In our own day, we witness remarkable movements—both the return of Israel to her land and the explosive growth of the global church—as signposts pointing toward the fulfillment of ancient oracles. This chapter explores how Israel's unique calling anchors the ingathering of the nations, how Jewish and Gentile believers are woven together into one family, and how history's greatest restoration foreshadows the eternal unity we will enjoy around the throne of the Lamb.

7.1 Covenantal Foundations

7.1.1 Abrahamic Promise of Blessing

God's promise to Abraham in Genesis 12:1–3 laid the groundwork for Israel's unique role in redemptive history. When God said, "In you all the families of the earth shall be blessed," He tied Abraham's seed to a universal purpose that transcended ethnic borders. The immediate fulfillment came through Isaac and Jacob, but the fuller realization awaited the coming Messiah—Christ—who is the true seed (Galatians 3:16). By blessing Abraham, God established a covenant that would expand from a single family to a nation and ultimately to a redeemed world (Genesis 17:7). This divine pledge underscored that Israel's election was never for self-exaltation but to serve as a channel of grace to the nations (Deuteronomy 4:6). Through Abraham's lineage, the law was given to reveal human sinfulness and drive both Jew and Gentile to Christ's righteousness (Romans 3:20–22). Paul reminds us that those who have faith are children of Abraham, heirs to the promise of blessing (Galatians 3:7–9). Thus, the Abrahamic covenant is both particular—centering on one people—and universal—open to every nation by faith. Israel's story of election and restoration continually points back to this foundational promise, inviting the church to celebrate and extend it. In every generation, believers embody Abraham's faith by trusting God's word and participating in His mission to bless the world.

7.1.2 Mosaic Law as Light to the Gentiles

When God gave the Law at Sinai, He explained that Israel's obedience would serve as a living example to the nations: "You shall be to me a kingdom of priests and a holy nation" (Exodus 19:6). The Torah codified moral, civil, and ceremonial statutes that showcased God's character—His justice, mercy, and holiness (Leviticus 19:2; Micah 6:8). Foreigners who lived among Israel could observe these laws and, under certain provisions, join the community by practicing justice and worshiping the true God (Exodus 12:48). Israel's annual festivals—Passover, Pentecost, Tabernacles—drew sojourners and emissaries from neighboring lands, providing opportunities to hear Yahweh's fame and redemptive acts (Deuteronomy 16:11; 31:12). The prophets later lamented Israel's failure to be a light when they forsook justice, yet held out hope that a restored nation would draw the Gentiles back to worship (Isaiah 49:6; 56:6–8). Paul interprets the Law as a tutor leading to Christ, showing both Jews and Gentiles their need for grace (Galatians 3:24). Even after Christ's advent, the moral imperatives of the Law continue to instruct the church in righteous living (Romans 13:8–10). In missionary contexts, Old Testament narratives often provide accessible windows into God's dealings, proving the Law's ongoing pedagogical value. The pattern of covenant obligations and blessings in Deuteronomy prefigures the church's call to demonstrate God's kingdom on earth. By living out the Law's underlying principles of love and justice, believers offer the nations a compelling foretaste of the coming reign.

7.1.3 Davidic Kingship and Universal Reign

God's covenant with David included the promise that his throne would be established forever (2 Samuel 7:16), pointing ahead to the Messiah's eternal reign. Psalm 72, attributed to Solomon, envisions a king whose rule extends to the ends of the earth, bringing justice and peace to all nations (Psalm 72:8–11). In the New Testament, the angel Gabriel tells Mary that her Son "will be great...and of his kingdom there will be no end" (Luke 1:32–33). Jesus frequently applied Davidic titles to Himself—Son of David—affirming His messianic identity (Matthew 21:9; 22:42–45). The early church preached that Jesus, raised from the dead, was installed at God's right hand to rule the nations until every enemy is subdued (Acts 2:29–36; 1 Corinthians 15:25). Revelation depicts Christ as King of kings and Lord of lords, coming on a white horse to execute justice and establish His universal dominion (Revelation 19:16). This kingship transcends geopolitical boundaries, encompassing every tribe and tongue (Revelation 5:9–10). In light of David's covenant, the church prays "Your kingdom come" as an invocation of Christ's already inaugurated yet awaiting consummated reign (Matthew 6:10). Believers thus live under the rule of the Davidic King, anticipating the day when "He will have dominion from sea to sea" (Psalm 72:8). Meanwhile, the church participates in His reign by advancing justice, proclaiming mercy, and embodying the kingdom values of humility and service (Matthew 20:28).

7.2 Prophetic Promises of Regathering

7.2.1 Isaiah's Vision of a Multiethnic Worship

Isaiah foresaw a future when "many peoples shall come, and say, 'Come, let us go up to the mountain of the LORD...that he may teach us his ways, and that we may walk in his paths'" (Isaiah 2:2–3). This prophetic summit symbolizes Zion as the center of worship and instruction for all nations. The Servant Songs in Isaiah 42, 49, 50, and 52–53 describe a figure— Israel and ultimately the Messiah—who brings justice to the nations without resorting to violence (Isaiah 42:1–4). Isaiah 56 extends the invitation to foreigners and eunuchs, declaring that "the sons of the foreigner...I will bring to my holy mountain" if they cling to God and keep His covenant (Isaiah 56:6–7). This broad inclusion signals a spiritual regathering that transcends ethnic Israel, anticipating the church's international character. Isaiah's temple vision (Isaiah 66:18– 23) portrays nations bringing their glory and offering worship, foreshadowing Revelation's picture of a redeemed, multiethnic assembly (Revelation 7:9–10). The prophet's call for righteousness and peace underscores that true worship requires ethical transformation (Isaiah 1:16–17). In this vision, Israel's restoration and the nations' ingathering are inseparable, each completing God's purposes. Contemporary believers draw encouragement from Isaiah's portrayal, knowing that God's mission always involves both justice and joyful celebration. Ultimately, Isaiah's prophecies invite the church to join in building a worshiping community that reflects heaven's diversity.

7.2.2 Jeremiah's New Covenant and Heart Renewal

Jeremiah prophesied a new covenant distinct from the Mosaic, one "I will put my law within them, and I will write it on their hearts" (Jeremiah 31:33). This promise of internal transformation addresses the failure of external codes to produce lasting faithfulness (Jeremiah 31:32). In the same passage, God declares that He will forgive iniquity and remember sin no more (Jeremiah 31:34), highlighting the mercy at the heart of the new covenant. The prophet also foresaw foreigners who "join themselves to the LORD" being brought to Jerusalem as part of the covenant community (Jeremiah 12:15). This anticipates Paul's teaching that through Christ, Jew and Gentile become one new man (Ephesians 2:14–16). The writer of Hebrews cites Jeremiah's new covenant to show Christ's priestly sacrifice secures this promise (Hebrews 8:8–13). Heart renewal signals that true ingathering depends on regenerated lives, not merely geographic relocation. The church's task is to witness to this transformative gospel, offering living water and Spirit baptism (John 7:37–39). Jeremiah's vision thus grounds global unity in divine initiative, not human diplomacy. By embracing the new covenant, both Jewish and Gentile believers experience belonging and share in the life-giving presence of God.

7.2.3 Ezekiel's Dry Bones and Vision of Restoration

Ezekiel's dramatic vision of a valley full of dry bones powerfully depicts Israel's national resurrection: "Behold, I will cause breath to enter you, and you shall live" (Ezekiel 37:5). The prophecy unfolds in stages: the bones assemble, flesh covers them, and breath brings them to life, symbolizing God's comprehensive restoration (Ezekiel 37:7–10). The two-stick vision that follows—one for Judah and one for Joseph— signifies the reunification of Israel and the healing of long-standing divisions (Ezekiel 37:15–22). God promises to make them one nation under one king, planting them in their own land (Ezekiel 37:24–25). This unity finds deeper fulfillment in Christ, the true Shepherd-King whose reign unites believers from every background (John 10:14–16). Ezekiel's restoration includes an emphasis on holiness—ritual purity and spiritual fidelity—preparing a people fit for divine habitation (Ezekiel 36:25–27). The valley of dry bones captures both physical and spiritual exile, addressing the scattering of Israel and the diaspora's longing to return. It also prefigures the church's own journey from death in sin to resurrection in Christ (Romans 6:4). Contemporary interpreters draw hope from Ezekiel's promise, believing that no situation is too hopeless for God's life-giving word. In the grand narrative, the dry bones echo until every knee bows and every voice confesses the Lordship of Jesus (Philippians 2:10–11).

7.3 Historic and Modern Regathering

7.3.1 Exiles Returning: Babylon to Jerusalem

When Cyrus the Persian issued his edict in 538 BC permitting Jewish exiles to return, Scripture declares, "Thus says Cyrus king of Persia: The LORD, the God of heaven, has given me all the kingdoms of the earth...he has charged me to build him a house at Jerusalem" (Ezra 1:2). This remarkable decree fulfilled Isaiah's prophecy nearly a century earlier (Isaiah 44:28), demonstrating God's sovereign orchestration of empires for His purposes. Under Zerubbabel's leadership, exiles rebuilt the temple, and later Nehemiah oversaw the restoration of Jerusalem's walls despite fierce opposition (Nehemiah 2:17–18; 6:1–9). Prophets Haggai and Zechariah encouraged the people not only to reconstruct structures but to trust in God's presence and future glory (Haggai 2:4–9; Zechariah 4:6–10). This first return was partial and fraught with compromise, yet it became a living testimony to God's faithfulness even after generations in captivity. The restored community observed the Passover anew, marking a fresh covenantal beginning (Ezra 6:19–22). These events set a pattern: physical return and spiritual renewal go hand in hand. For the church today, the Babylon-to-Jerusalem story exemplifies how God can transform exile into mission and oppression into opportunity. The historic return also prefigures the ultimate gathering of the redeemed at the Lord's return. Believers draw courage from this narrative when facing metaphorical exiles in hostile cultures.

7.3.2 Scattering of the Diaspora

Before and after the Babylonian exile, Israel experienced multiple deportations—Assyrians in the 8th century BC and Romans in AD 70—resulting in Jewish communities spread across the Mediterranean and beyond (2 Kings 17:6; Luke 21:20–24). These diasporic Jews often maintained their distinct identity through synagogue worship, Sabbath observance, and dietary laws (Ezra 1:3; Acts 2:5–11). The dispersion ironically facilitated God's global purposes by positioning Jewish witnesses in every major city of the Roman world, priming the soil for the gospel's spread (Acts 8:1; 11:19). Paul's missionary journeys traced these roads of exile, reaching both Jews and God-fearing Gentiles (Acts 13–18). The enduring faith of diaspora communities—despite isolation and persecution—speaks to the power of God to sustain His people without political backing. Holocaust survivors and modern immigrants continue that legacy, often integrating deep spiritual resilience with active missionary outreach. Messianic Jewish movements today testify to the diaspora's ongoing role in bridging Jewish tradition and gospel proclamation. The scattering has thus become a means of divine strategy, echoing Joseph's words: "You meant evil against me, but God meant it for good" (Genesis 50:20). In diaspora contexts, the church learns to worship under adversity and to carry God's presence wherever they arrive.

7.3.3 Zionism and Spiritual Awakening

The rise of Zionism in the late 19th and early 20th centuries, motivated by both political and religious convictions, led to Jewish immigration to Palestine, culminating in the establishment of the modern state of Israel in 1948. Many evangelicals view this as a partial fulfillment of Ezekiel's dry bones prophecy (Ezekiel 37:12–14) and God's promise to regather His people (Isaiah 11:11–12). Alongside political Zionism, spiritual movements have emerged—Jewish believers in Yeshua (Messianic Jews) and Jewish-renewal groups seeking spiritual rediscovery of covenant faith. These awakenings highlight that regathering is not merely demographic but deeply spiritual, involving recognition of the

Messiah and repentance (Romans 11:25–26). Contemporary surveys indicate that increasing numbers of Jews worldwide are exploring Jesus as the Jewish Messiah, reflecting a spiritual ingathering alongside the physical. Messianic congregations in Israel and the diaspora serve as living bridges between Jewish tradition and Christian faith. The ingathering witnessed today mirrors biblical patterns: return to the land accompanied by revival of heart (Deuteronomy 30:3–6). Tensions and controversies swirl around these developments, yet they underscore that God's purposes transcend human politics. Ultimately, Zionism and spiritual awakening point toward the climactic day when Israel's Messiah will be universally acknowledged (Zechariah 12:10). The church observes these converging currents with prayerful expectation, knowing that every element contributes to God's unfolding plan.

7.4 Spiritual Ingathering of Israel

7.4.1 Paul's Olive Tree Imagery

In Romans 11, Paul likens Israel to a cultivated olive tree into which Gentile branches have been grafted, warning against arrogance by the Gentile believers: "you do not support the root, but the root supports you" (Romans 11:18). His metaphor underscores that the natural branches—ethnic Israel—were broken off because of unbelief (Romans 11:20), yet a remnant was kept by grace (Romans 11:5). Gentile inclusion demonstrates God's patience and purpose "to make [Israel] jealous" (Romans 11:11), driving them to seek the true olive shoot, Christ. Paul then promises that if Israel does not persist in unbelief, "they will be grafted in" again—"for God has the power to graft them in again" (Romans 11:23). The olive tree thus symbolizes God's one people across ages: root in Israel, wild branches in the nations, all nourished by divine grace. This picture affirms that God's covenant promises to Israel remain irrevocable even as He extends covenant blessings to Gentiles (Romans 11:29). Paul concludes with doxology: "Oh, the depth of the riches and wisdom and knowledge of God!...For from him and through him and to him are all things"

(Romans 11:33, 36), celebrating the mystery of this ingathering. The imagery calls believers to humility, mutual dependence, and hope for Israel's full restoration. It also provides a theological framework for Jewish–Gentile unity in the church. As the olive tree flourishes only by receiving life from its root, so the global church thrives by remaining connected to Israel's covenant heritage and Christ's messianic mission.

7.4.2 A Remnant According to Grace

Throughout Scripture, God preserves a believing remnant—even when the majority falls into idolatry or unbelief. Isaiah wrote of the "holy seed" that constitutes a remnant after judgment (Isaiah 6:13). In the post-exilic period, only a fraction returned to Jerusalem, yet they formed the nucleus for renewed covenant community (Ezra 2:64–65). In New Testament times, Peter declares that "the Lord knows how to rescue the godly from trials," echoing Elijah's story of 7,000 faithful in Israel (1 Peter 1:5; 1 Kings 19:18). Paul speaks of this remnant as "according to election" (Romans 11:5), emphasizing divine initiative over human merit. This remnant experiences heart transformation by the Spirit, fulfilling Jeremiah's new covenant promise of "I will put my law within them" (Jeremiah 31:33). God's preservation of a remnant underscores His sovereign faithfulness—He does not abandon His people even in their unfaithfulness (Deuteronomy 31:6). Contemporary Messianic Jewish congregations often see themselves as part of this remnant, carrying both Jewish identity and faith in Yeshua the Messiah. Their existence testifies to the continuity of God's covenant plan and invites the wider church to honor and learn from this heritage. Recognizing the remnant's role helps believers appreciate the interplay of divine election, human responsibility, and missionary partnership in God's regathering work.

7.4.3 Jewish Believers and Messianic Communities

The earliest Christian communities were primarily Jewish—Acts 2 describes 3,000 Jews converted at Pentecost, meeting in Solomon's Portico (Acts 2:41–46). As the gospel spread, Gentiles joined, but the Jerusalem church continued temple worship and Jewish practices (Acts 21:20), illustrating the initial unity of Jewish and Gentile believers. Over time, Gentile expressions of faith developed distinct forms, yet Jewish believers maintained a foothold in missions, letter writing, and theological reflection (Romans 16). Today, Messianic Jewish congregations blend Jewish liturgy, Scripture readings from the Tanakh, and rejoicing in Yeshua as Messiah. This hybrid identity honors ancestral traditions while embracing the universal scope of salvation (Ephesians 2:14–18). These communities face unique challenges: navigating Jewish communal opposition, clarifying theological distinctions, and maintaining cultural authenticity without isolation. Yet they also offer powerful testimony to both Jews and Gentiles— Jewish believers bear witness to the Messiah's Jewish roots, while Gentile churches learn the Hebraic foundations of faith (Romans 9:4–5). Partnerships between Messianic congregations and historical churches enrich global mission, sharing insights into contextual evangelism among Jewish people. Their existence exemplifies the reconciliation Paul spoke of: "Christ has broken down the dividing wall...the two have become one new man" (Ephesians 2:14–15). As spiritual bridges, they point toward the coming day when Israel's fullness will number as many as the sand (Romans 11:26), fulfilling God's promise to His ancient people.

7.5 Gentile Inclusion and Global Mission

7.5.1 Great Commission's Mandate

Jesus charged His disciples to "go and make disciples of all nations" (Matthew 28:19), extending the Abrahamic blessing to every people group. This universal mandate picks up Isaiah's call for the nations to seek the Lord (Isaiah 2:2–3) and Jeremiah's vision of foreigners joining God's covenant (Jeremiah 12:15). Pentecost fulfilled the initial phase, as devout Jews from "every nation under heaven" heard the apostles in their own languages (Acts 2:5–11). The Great Commission involves baptizing in the name of the triune God and teaching obedience to Christ's commands—a holistic process of formation (Matthew 28:20). It underscores that baptism into Christ erases ethnic divisions: "There is neither Jew nor Greek...for you are all one in Christ Jesus" (Galatians 3:28). The early church pursued this mission amid persecution, famine, and political upheaval, demonstrating that suffering and proclamation often go hand in hand (Acts 8:1; 11:19–21). The Great Commission remains the church's driving purpose, guiding evangelism strategies, cross–cultural partnerships, and diaspora ministry. It also provides the eschatological framework: as the nations respond, they prepare the way for Christ's return (Matthew 24:14). Believers today engage this mandate through local outreach, global partnerships, and prayer for unreached peoples, reflecting the church's ongoing participation in God's covenant mission.

7.5.2 Paul's Missionary Strategy

Paul's missionary approach combined urban focus, strategic partnerships, and contextual sensitivity: he "went into the Jewish synagogue" first, reasoning with both Jews and Greeks (Acts 17:1–4). His pattern of founding a strong local church—appointing elders, teaching Scripture, and fostering indigenous leadership—ensured sustainability (Titus 1:5; Acts 14:23). Paul contextualized the gospel without compromise: he "became all things to all people, that by all means he might save some" (1 Corinthians 9:22). He avoided imposing Jewish ceremonial laws on Gentiles, convening the Jerusalem Council to affirm freedom in Christ (Acts 15:1–29). His epistles provided theological grounding, ethical instruction, and corporate unity across diverse cultures. He emphasized prayer support from home churches (Colossians 4:2–4), recognizing intercession as vital to mission success. Paul also leveraged his Roman citizenship for witness before governors and kings (Acts 25:11), demonstrating the interplay of spiritual boldness and astute use of civic status. His mentorship of Timothy and Titus exemplified succession planning, equipping younger leaders to carry on the work (2 Timothy 2:2). Paul's multifaceted strategy offers a blueprint for contemporary mission: balance proclamation and contextualization, prioritize local empowerment, and ground efforts in prayer and theological clarity.

7.5.3 Contemporary Waves of Global Harvest

In recent decades, Asia, Africa, and Latin America have experienced remarkable church growth, often through grassroots movements and house–church networks. Countries once deemed "closed" to the gospel now report exponential growth, with millions coming to faith in contexts of persecution (Matthew 5:10–12). Prayer initiatives—such as the 10/40 Window focus—and Scripture translations using digital audio Bibles have accelerated access to the Word. Movements like the Jesus Film Project and Scripture union partnerships leverage media to introduce Christ in local languages. Indigenous-led church–planting movements prioritize rapid multiplication through lay leadership and simple reproducible models (Matthew 28:19–20). Organizations report that some of the fastest–growing churches worldwide require no building, formal liturgy, or paid clergy—just a group of believers studying Scripture, praying, and sharing testimonies. This "fractal church" model reflects New Testament patterns in Acts and Paul's letters (Acts 5:42; Romans 16). Revival waves—such as those in Korea, Brazil, and Sudan—underscore the synergistic effect of prayer, evangelistic outreach, and social transformation. These contemporary harvests demonstrate God's ongoing faithfulness to His promise: that every nation will be represented before His throne (Revelation 7:9–10).

7.6 Millennial Unity and Eternal Fellowship

7.6.1 Millennial Reign Centered in Jerusalem

Revelation 20 describes Christ's millennial reign, during which Satan is bound and the saints reign with Him for a thousand years (Revelation 20:1–6). This reign echoes Old Testament prophecies of peace emanating from Zion: "They shall beat their swords into plowshares...and learn war no more" (Isaiah 2:4). Jerusalem functions as the judicial and worship capital, with nations streaming to learn God's ways (Micah 4:1–3). Ezekiel's millennial temple vision provides architectural and liturgical details for worship centrality (Ezekiel 40–48). The binding of Satan ensures that Christ's rule is uncontested, enabling the full realization of kingdom righteousness and healing of creation (Romans 8:19–23). Saints govern with Christ, reflecting the believer's participation in His victory and reign (2 Timothy 2:12). This millennial scene foreshadows the New Heavens and New Earth, serving as a transitional phase of restoration. Jerusalem's role underscores God's faithfulness to His original choice of Zion as the place of divine residence (Psalm 132:13–14). Believers today live in light of this millennial hope, engaging in earthly justice ministries with an eye to eternal fulfillment. The millennial reign thus unites Israel and the nations under Christ's benevolent sovereignty.

7.6.2 New Heavens, New Earth, New Jerusalem

At the close of redemptive history, Revelation unveils the descent of the New Jerusalem from heaven—a city adorned like a bride, coming to earth (Revelation 21:2). This city symbolizes God dwelling among people, wiping away every tear, and abolishing death, mourning, crying, and pain (Revelation 21:3–4). Its twelve gates—named for the twelve tribes—and twelve foundations—named for the twelve apostles—uniquely blend Israel's and the church's identities (Revelation 21:12–14). The river of life flows from God's throne, with the tree of life on its banks bearing fruit for the healing of the nations (Revelation 22:1–2), fulfilling Genesis 2 while transcending Eden. No temple is needed, for "the Lord God the Almighty and the Lamb are its temple" (Revelation 21:22), uniting worshipers in direct communion. The open gates signify perpetual access for the nations, eliminating any barrier to fellowship (Revelation 21:25). The radiance of the city—reflecting God's glory—provides all needed light, rendering sun and moon obsolete (Revelation 21:23). This vision consummates the theme of ingathering: all peoples share equal citizenship in the heavenly city (Philippians 3:20).

It inspires present–day faithfulness, reminding the church that every act of service and worship contributes to the eternal community. Thus, the New Jerusalem becomes both goal and catalyst for joyful, hope–filled mission.

7.6.3 Living as Foretaste of the Ingathering

Even before the consummation, the church is called to embody the coming unity by practicing hospitality, reconciliation, and justice. The New Covenant commands believers to "welcome one another, as Christ has welcomed you" (Romans 15:7), mirroring the open gates of the New Jerusalem. Corporate worship that incorporates diverse languages, music, and cultural expressions prefigures the heavenly chorus (Revelation 7:9–10). Acts of mercy—feeding the hungry, caring for refugees, advocating for the imprisoned—anticipate the Lamb's justice and compassion (Matthew 25:35–40). Intercultural partnerships and codeveloped ministries demonstrate the power of cross–ethnic unity (Ephesians 4:3). Prayer networks mobilize the global body to intercede for unreached peoples, aligning earthly action with heavenly vision (Isaiah 56:7). Small–group fellowships that span generational and ethnic lines provide tangible foretaste of the family described in Galatians 3:28. Educational initiatives that teach biblical theology alongside cultural understanding equip believers to navigate diversity with wisdom. By living as a foretaste, the church testifies that the barriers dividing humanity are shattered in Christ (Colossians 2:14). These present realities point the world to the coming age when every nation will rejoice in the unity and glory of God.

Conclusion

As God's covenant people and His worldwide mission converge, we see that no cultural barrier or political boundary can thwart His resolve to draw all men and women into fellowship with Himself. The ingathering of Israel and the embrace of the Gentiles in Christ together signal the dawn of a new humanity—one that transcends divisions and reflects the diversity of God's creative genius. In standing at this pivotal moment, the church is called to model that unity now: welcoming Jewish and Gentile brothers and sisters, partnering in gospel proclamation, and anticipating the day when every nation will worship as one before the New Jerusalem. May this vision stir our hearts to live as foretaste of that eternal gathering, embodying mercy, justice, and love until the King returns to claim His people and consummate the promise of unending fellowship.

Chapter 8. The Glorious Appearing of the King

When the ages draw to a close, the heavens themselves will proclaim the arrival of their Maker in a spectacle no eye can miss. Christ's second advent is neither a whisper nor a hidden event—it will break into history with cosmic fanfare, trumpets of God, and the voice of the archangel calling His people to rise. In that decisive moment, death and decay will give way to resurrection life, and the one who once conquered sin through the cross will demonstrate His unchallenged authority over every power of darkness. This glorious appearing is the culmination of every promise, prophecy, and prayer—the day when the faithful remnant hears "Well done" and the nations witness the restoration of all things under the sovereign King.

8.1 Descent with Shout and Trumpet

8.1.1 "Every Eye Shall See Him"

Scripture assures us that Christ's return will not be a secret rapture unseen by the world, but a universally visible event:

"Behold, he is coming with the clouds, and every eye will see him" (Revelation 1:7). This promise echoes Jesus' own words, "then will appear in heaven the sign of the Son of Man...and all the tribes of the earth will mourn" (Matthew 24:30). The cosmic disturbances that precede His coming—sun darkened, moon turned to blood—serve to grab the attention of every living creature (Joel 2:31; Luke 21:25–26). Unbelievers will wail, "Woe to us!" as they recognize too late the Lord of glory arriving in righteous judgment. Yet for the faithful, this universal unveiling brings no terror but the joy of "with the clouds of heaven" being caught up to meet the Lord (1 Thessalonians 4:17). The worldwide visibility underscores that God's salvific purposes are public and transformative: no corner of creation will be untouched by His presence. Art and literature throughout history have grappled with this motif, portraying skies ablaze or armies halted by an unearthly light. Theologians observe that such a revelation demolishes every idol—political, economic, or religious—as all will see the true King. Finally, the global spectacle affirms the integrity of God's word: He who spoke the world into being will one day make His second coming as undeniable as creation itself.

8.1.2 The Loud Command and Archangel's Voice

Paul records that at the Lord's return "the dead in Christ will rise first. Then we who are alive...will be caught up...at the sound of the trumpet of God—for the Lord himself will descend from heaven with a cry of command, with the voice of an archangel, and with the sound of the trumpet of God" (1 Thessalonians 4:16). This triple announcement—the echoing shout, the archangel's voice, and the trumpet blast—highlights the authoritative summons that rouses both saints and sleepers. In the Old Testament, angelic voices frequently accompanied divine revelation, such as the "mighty voice" at Sinai that struck the people with fear (Exodus 19:19). The shout of command recalls Ezekiel's vision of the whirlwind and the living creatures, where heaven's voice initiates cosmic movement (Ezekiel 1:24). The archangel Michael is elsewhere depicted as contending with demonic forces (Daniel 10:13) and standing for Israel, reinforcing the martial and protective dimensions of the announcement. Trumpets in Israelite tradition signaled sacred assemblies, war alarms, and jubilee proclamations (Leviticus 25:9; Numbers 10:1–10), all foreshadowing the ultimate gathering under Christ's lordship. Together, these elements convey that the resurrection and rapture are more than physical events—they are a divine decree that cannot be ignored. Believers are thus urged to maintain spiritual readiness, heeding the call as though "at an hour you do not expect" (Matthew 24:44). The convergence of command, angelic voice, and trumpet underscores that no mere human proclamation can match this unparalleled, triune announcement.

8.1.3 The Last Trumpet's Call

Paul describes the climactic moment of transformation: "For the trumpet will sound, and the dead will be raised imperishable, and we shall be changed" (1 Corinthians 15:52). This "last trumpet" parallels the Jubilee trumpet that heralded liberty and restoration every fiftieth year (Leviticus 25:9), pointing to ultimate freedom from sin and death. The perishable putting on the imperishable echoes the Seed–Sower parable: just as a seed transforms when planted, so our mortal bodies will rise uncorrupted (1 Corinthians 15:35–44). In prophetic literature, trumpets also announce the Day of the Lord—an era of both judgment and deliverance (Zephaniah 1:14; Amos 3:6). The Levitical soundings guided Israel's worship and warfare, reinforcing that God's people mobilize by divine command, not human will (Numbers 10:2–5). The apostolic emphasis on this trumpet encourages perseverance, for the transformation it brings is both sudden and glorious. Early church creeds included lines about the trumpet call, embedding this future hope into weekly worship. Modern hymns such as "The Trumpet Shall Sound" draw directly on Paul's language, reinforcing the connection between biblical prophecy and Christian hope. Ultimately, the last trumpet summons creation to its climax—death conquered, Christ's body glorified, and His Bride made ready for eternal fellowship.

8.2 Resurrection and Transformation

8.2.1 Raising the Righteous Dead

Jesus declared Himself "the resurrection and the life" (John 11:25), grounding Christian hope in His own rising from the grave. Paul affirms that Christ is the firstfruits of those who have fallen asleep, and that His resurrection guarantees ours in due order: "Christ the firstfruits, then at his coming those who belong to Christ" (1 Corinthians 15:23). The righteous dead will rise with bodies suited for the eternal glory—immortal, imperishable, and free from the decay that marks our present flesh (1 Corinthians 15:42–44). Daniel's prophecy speaks of many who "sleep in the dust of the earth [who] shall awake, some to everlasting life" (Daniel 12:2), showing that Jewish hope of bodily resurrection finds its fullest expression in Christ. The dead in Christ rise first, affirming that salvation always begins with divine initiative, not human striving (Ephesians 2:8–9). This resurrection removes the sting of death, for "death has been swallowed up in victory" (1 Corinthians 15:54). The apocalyptic imagery of white robes and resurrection throngs in Revelation (Revelation 20:4–6) echoes this triumphant outcome. Each believer's identity is thus secured: though we sleep in death for a time, our future body awaits in the hands of the Creator (Matthew 10:28). The certainty of resurrection transforms how Christians view mortality—no longer as an end but as a passage to a more glorious existence (Philippians 1:23). By raising the righteous dead first, God underscores that His justice and mercy culminate in eternal life for all who belong to Christ.

8.2.2 Transfiguration of the Living

Paul continues, "We who are alive, who are left, will be caught up together with them in the clouds to meet the Lord in the air, and so we will always be with the Lord" (1 Thessalonians 4:17). This promise applies to those alive at His appearing, who will undergo instantaneous transfiguration—"we shall be changed…in a moment, in the twinkling of an eye" (1 Corinthians 15:52). The language of "putting on" immortality and imperishability (1 Corinthians 15:53) evokes Christ's glorified body, which bore the marks of crucifixion yet shone with resurrection life (John 20:20). The mysterious nature of this change underscores that glorified existence transcends current biological constraints. Jesus' transfiguration on the mountain (Matthew 17:2) served as a preview of this transformation, showing disciples a glimpse of His divine glory. The transfiguration of the living ensures no believer misses the resurrection wave—those alive and remaining experience divine glorification without tasting death. This hope combats the fear of death and the ennui of aging, for no matter our earthly condition, Christ's appearing brings new life. Early hymns reference this change, celebrating the transformation of our "weak mortal frame" (Isaiah 40:29). The instantaneous nature—"twinkling of an eye"—also warns against complacency: readiness must be constant, since the timing remains known only to the Father (Matthew 24:36). Ultimately, the living are drawn into the cosmic redemption at the very moment of Christ's descent, highlighting the inseparable union between Christ and His body the church.

8.2.3 Union with the Bridegroom

Scripture portrays the church as the Bride of Christ, prepared for union at His return: "He who has the bride is the bridegroom" (John 3:29). Jesus taught His disciples to desire that day when He would take His people to be with Him (John 14:3), undergirding the marriage metaphor with promises of indwelling presence. The wedding imagery recalls prophetic anticipations in Isaiah's songs of new covenant intimacy (Isaiah 54:5–6). Paul reinforces this by describing the church's sanctification as a presenting of "the bride without spot or wrinkle" (Ephesians 5:27). At the rapture, the Bridegroom's shout heralds the wedding procession—He will gather His Bride to Himself, fulfilling the "marriage supper of the Lamb" (Revelation 19:7–9). The relational depth extends beyond mere fellowship; it is a covenant reunion echoing "two shall become one flesh" (Ephesians 5:31). Jesus' promise that "I will not leave you as orphans" (John 14:18) finds ultimate fulfillment in this marriage, where abandonment is forever banished. The imagery reminds believers that union with

123

Christ is both mystical and concrete—a future, physical gathering that reflects present spiritual communion through the Spirit. This coming wedding stirs the church to worship with anticipation, shaping liturgies that anticipate the Lamb's banquet. In union with the Bridegroom, the church enters its highest calling: to love and to be loved by the One who gave Himself for her (Ephesians 5:25–26).

8.3 Vanquishing Evil

8.3.1 Defeat of the Beast and False Prophet

Revelation 19 portrays the climactic confrontation at Christ's appearing: "I saw the beast and the kings of the earth with their armies... and I saw the beast and the false prophet... and they were thrown alive into the lake of fire" (Revelation 19:19–20). The beast, symbolizing political tyranny, and the false prophet, representing religious deception, together form the satanic power structure opposing Christ's reign. Their public humiliation demonstrates that every counterfeit authority drains its power at the foot of the Lamb (Psalm 2:1–4). The imagery of being thrown alive into the lake of fire underscores the finality and personal accountability inherent in divine justice. This defeat fulfills Daniel's prophecy that the Ancient of Days "shall put the beast to the ban" (Daniel 7:26). The saints' vindication—clothed in white and rejoicing—contrasts sharply with the beast's ignominious end, affirming that loyalty to Christ leads to honor rather than shame (Revelation 7:13–14). Revelation's narrative weaves this overthrow into the broader metanarrative of God's redemptive plan, marking the end of human rebellion. Liturgies often incorporate passages from Revelation 19 to celebrate Christ's victory as a foretaste of His coming judgment. Believers draw courage from this assurance when facing present spiritual opposition, knowing that the ultimate outcome is never in doubt. The defeat of the beast and false prophet thus declares that no evil—political, religious, or cultural—can withstand the sword of the Word (Hebrews 4:12).

8.3.2 Binding of Satan

Immediately following the beast's overthrow, Revelation recounts: "I saw an angel...seize the dragon...and bind him for a thousand years" (Revelation 20:1–2). Satan, the ancient serpent, is cast down from heaven (Revelation 12:9) and imprisoned, preventing him from deceiving the nations during the millennium. This binding fulfills Isaiah's prophecy that the Lord would "bind up the strong man" before plundering his house (Isaiah 49:24–25), illustrating Christ's authority over demonic powers. The thousand-year period of restraint allows Christ's peaceable kingdom to flourish without hindrance, reflecting Ezekiel's vision of a peaceful reign where "they shall lie down safely" (Ezekiel 34:25). Saints reigning with Christ experience this deliverance firsthand, administering justice under His oversight. The binding also underscores that earthly conflicts have spiritual origins, and resolving them requires divine intervention (Ephesians 6:12–13). After the millennium, Satan's brief release tests the nations one last time, demonstrating that only those whose names are written in the Lamb's book have true loyalty. The angelic binding thus affirms that Christ's victory on the cross extends to cosmic reconciliation, guaranteeing a season of peace and righteousness. Believers today pray for spiritual breakthroughs anticipating this binding, engaging in warfare prayer with confidence in Christ's ultimate supremacy. The binding of Satan is therefore both a future promise and a present assurance of Christ's dominion over dark forces.

8.3.3 Destruction of the Armies at Armageddon

Revelation 16's sixth bowl gathers the nations for the great battle at the place called Armageddon: "Then they assembled the kings...to the place that in Hebrew is called Armageddon" (Revelation 16:16). This symbolic site—har-Magedon, or Mount of Megiddo—has long been associated with military encounters in Israel's history (Judges 4–5), signifying decisive conflict. The eschatological battle culminates not in human victory but in Christ's swift destruction of His enemies: "by the word of his mouth...and the breath of his lips he will kill the wicked" (2 Thessalonians 2:8). The combination of divine word and breath echoes Isaiah's imagery of judgment and vindication (Isaiah 11:4). Revelation 19 depicts Christ as a warrior on a white horse, "with eyes like a flame of fire...and on his robe and on his thigh he has a name written, King of kings and Lord of lords" (Revelation 19:12–16). This portrayal assures the faithful that every attempt to oppose God's kingdom ends in defeat, not by human effort but by divine ordinance. The armies of the beast—a coalition of political, economic, and religious powers—are utterly routed, illustrating that false alliances cannot stand before truth (Zechariah 14:3). The destruction of these forces vindicates all who suffered under their tyranny, affirming God's commitment to justice (Revelation 6:9–11). For the remnant, Armageddon stands as a reminder that perseverance in faith, even amid overwhelming odds, culminates in vindication and peace. Thus, the cosmic battle at Armageddon transitions history from tribulation to triumph under Christ's reign.

8.4 Wedding Supper of the Lamb

8.4.1 Preparation of the Bride

Long before the Lamb's return, Scripture depicts the church as a bride being prepared for her wedding day. Ephesians 5:25–27 likens Christ's cleansing work to purifying the church "that he might present the church to himself in splendor, without spot or wrinkle." This process begins in this age through sanctification by the Spirit (1 Thessalonians 4:3) and continues through trials that refine our faith (1 Peter 1:6–7). Revelation 19:7–8 portrays the bride clothed in "fine linen, bright and clean," a symbol of the "righteous deeds of the saints." Jewish wedding customs required a period of betrothal, during which the bride prepared her wedding garments—symbolizing readiness and purity (Song of Solomon 2:4). In the same way, believers adorn themselves with virtues like love, joy, and peace as evidence of the Spirit's work (Galatians 5:22–23). Corporate worship and the sacraments serve as rehearsals, strengthening communal identity and reminding us of the promised union (1 Corinthians 11:26). Spiritual disciplines—Bible study, prayer, fellowship—

deepen intimacy with the Groom, ensuring we are ready when He appears (Revelation 3:20). The anticipation of the marriage supper motivates holy living: "So you also must consider yourselves dead to sin and alive to God in Christ Jesus" (Romans 6:11). Preparation of the bride, then, is both personal and communal, rooted in grace and expressed in faithful obedience until the great day.

8.4.2 Invitation Extended to the Faithful

The imagery of the marriage supper of the Lamb includes an explicit invitation: "Blessed are those who are invited to the marriage supper of the Lamb!" (Revelation 19:9). This call extends first to the faithful remnant—those who have persevered in holiness and love (Matthew 25:10–12). Jesus' parable of the wedding feast warns against complacency: those without wedding garments are cast out, illustrating the necessity of responding properly to the invitation (Matthew 22:1–14). The early church viewed every eucharistic celebration as participation in that coming banquet, proclaiming Christ's death "until he comes" (1 Corinthians 11:26). In Revelation 3:20, Christ stands at the door and knocks, offering fellowship to all who hear His voice—an echo of the marriage call. The invitation presupposes response: ignoring or rejecting it brings exclusion (Luke 14:24). Yet the invitation also carries grace: it is not earned by works but offered to all who trust in the Lamb (Romans 5:1). The Feast foreshadows the ultimate gathering of the redeemed from "every nation, tribe, people and language" (Revelation 7:9). Our participation in missional outreach mirrors this invitation, as we extend the gospel call globally (Matthew 28:19–20). Thus, the marriage supper's invitation underscores both God's sovereignty in calling and our responsibility to respond in faith and readiness.

8.4.3 The Joyful Union

When the marriage supper of the Lamb commences, believers experience consummate joy in union with Christ. Revelation 19:7 proclaims that "the marriage of the Lamb has come, and his Bride has made herself ready," emphasizing mutual delight. Old Testament imagery of God as bridegroom (Isaiah 62:5) captures the delight God takes in His people, mirrored now in the Lamb's rejoicing over His Bride (Zephaniah 3:17). Paul describes the mystery of Christ and the church as "profound" and "one flesh" in Ephesians 5:32, highlighting intimate unity. At the banquet, the community of the redeemed shares in the Lamb's victory and reign, symbolized by fellowship around His table (Luke 22:29–30). The joy of that day surpasses all earthly happiness: "Eye has not seen…what God has prepared for those who love him" (1 Corinthians 2:9). Worship in that moment will be unceasing, as "They will hunger no more, neither thirst anymore" (Revelation 7:16). The Lamb's marriage feast thus becomes the eternal culmination of covenant love, where every tear is wiped away (Revelation 21:4). This joyful union motivates present worship, as we sing "Alleluia! Salvation and glory and power belong to our God" (Revelation 19:1). The celebration reminds believers that all our hope rests not in circumstances but in the unfading joy of Christ's presence.

8.5 Judgment of the Nations

8.5.1 The Sheep and the Goats

Jesus' parable in Matthew 25:31–46 describes the Son of Man separating the nations as a shepherd separates sheep from goats. The sheep enter the kingdom by caring for the hungry, the thirsty, the stranger, the naked, the sick, and the imprisoned—acts of compassion rendered to Christ Himself (Matthew 25:40). The goats, by contrast, fail to serve "the least of these," and thus face condemnation (Matthew 25:45–46). This judgment highlights that authentic faith expresses itself in tangible love and service (James 2:17). The parable also underscores human responsibility: everyone hears the criteria and knows the call to mercy. The universal scope—"all the nations" (Matthew 25:32)—indicates that God judges every people group, not only individuals. The scene reveals that eschatological justice will be thorough and equitable, rewarding both generosity and neglect. This teaching confronts Christians with the reality that their works will be scrutinized, yet it offers hope that even small acts of kindness will be eternally significant. The parable's setting "at the end of the age" links acts of mercy with the consummation of history. It calls the church to integrate social compassion into gospel proclamation, anticipating the coming judgment of the nations.

8.5.2 Great White Throne Judgment

Revelation 20:11–15 depicts the final assize: "I saw a great white throne and him who was seated on it...the dead were judged by what was written in the books, according to what they had done." The opening of the Book of Life distinguishes those granted eternal life from those cast into the lake of fire. This judgment confirms that every deed, word, and thought is recorded—echoing Jesus' warning that nothing hidden will remain so (Matthew 12:36–37). The imagery of white highlights the purity and sovereignty of the Judge (Daniel 7:9). The fate of those not found in the Book of Life—the "second death" (Revelation 20:14)—emphasizes the finality of divine sentence. Yet this solemn scene affirms God's justice: He "will render to each one according to what he has done" (Romans 2:6). The disclosure of all works underscores that God's evaluation is comprehensive and fair. Martyn Lloyd-Jones observed that this vision impels evangelism, since so many will stand condemned without Christ (Romans 5:8). The hope of acquittal through faith in Christ becomes all the more precious when faced with this tribunal. The Great White Throne reminds believers of the urgency of the gospel for the nations and the accountability each person bears before the Creator.

8.5.3 Vindication of God's Justice

The final judgments—sheep and goats, white throne—serve a higher purpose: vindicating the justice and righteousness of God before all creation. Isaiah 66:16–24 describes that "by fire and by his sword will the LORD judge all flesh," culminating in the vindication of the righteous remnant. The harmony of mercy and judgment confirms that God's character is perfectly balanced; He punishes sin yet honors faithfulness (Psalm

96:13). The outpouring of justice silences any accusation that God is unjust or unconcerned (Romans 3:4). Revelation's cosmic courtroom brings every power—angelic, demonic, human—to acknowledge His right to govern (Philippians 2:10–11). The stories of the martyrs under the altar, crying for justice, receive their answer in these judgments (Revelation 6:9–11). Believers can trust that every tear and act of service will be weighed and appropriately rewarded (Revelation 22:12). As Augustine noted, "God's judgment is the ultimate proof of His holiness and love," since only an absolutely pure judge can eliminate evil once and for all. The vindication of God's justice also restores cosmic order, preparing for the eternal fellowship of a renewed creation (Revelation 21:1–4). Thus, final judgment is not a capricious act but the necessary restoration of righteousness for the sake of all who love Him.

8.6 Inauguration of the Eternal Kingdom

8.6.1 Coronation of the King

Following the overthrow of evil, Scripture depicts the enthronement of Christ as King of the renewed cosmos. Revelation 5:11–14 presents a heavenly chorus declaring, "Worthy is the Lamb who was slain, to receive power and wealth and wisdom and might and honor and glory and blessing!" This coronation echoes Psalm 2:6: "As for me, I have set my King on Zion, my holy hill." The title "King of kings and Lord of lords" (Revelation 19:16) asserts His supreme authority over all created powers. The coronation involves not only the Lamb but also the redeemed, who sing praises around the throne (Revelation 7:10). This scene fulfills Daniel's vision that the "Ancient of Days" would give "dominion and glory and a kingdom...to the Son of Man" (Daniel 7:13–14). The enthroned Christ judges the nations with equity, ensuring that His reign is characterized by justice and peace (Psalm 72:1–4). Doxologies throughout Scripture build toward this moment, as creation itself will declare His glory (Psalm 19:1). The coronation inaugurates the eternal reign that believers have awaited—and prayed for—since Jesus taught, "Your kingdom come" (Matthew 6:10). In this act, the only rightful Sovereign assumes His eternal throne, and all who bear His name rejoice in His victory.

8.6.2 Commencement of Millennial Reign

Revelation 20:4–6 describes the thousand–year reign of Christ with His saints, a period of peace, justice, and restoration on earth. During this millennial kingdom, Satan is bound, preventing further deception and ensuring the uninterrupted flourishing of God's rule. The saints "reign with Christ" as priests of God and of Christ, sharing in His authority (Revelation 20:6). This reign fulfills Isaiah's vision that the desert shall blossom and the wolf shall dwell with the lamb (Isaiah 35:1; 11:6). Ezekiel's millennial temple and river visions (Ezekiel 43–47) find partial realization as the earth is rejuvenated under the Messiah's governance. The resurrected and transformed saints administer righteous judgment, reflecting the kingly mediation of Christ (1 Corinthians 6:2–3). This reign is not a mere earthly utopia but a foretaste of New Heavens and New Earth, demonstrating God's restorative power (Revelation 21:1). The millennial promises also motivate present obedience and hope, as believers anticipate participation in Christ's kingdom work. Though interpretations vary, the core reality remains: God's people will experience His sovereign rule in fullness before eternity. Thus, the commencement of the millennial reign marks the transition from cosmic conflict to consummated peace.

8.6.3 From Triumph to Consummation

As the millennial reign concludes, Scripture points to the final transition into the eternal state—New Heavens, New Earth, and New Jerusalem. Revelation 21:1–4 describes the descent of the holy city, where God dwells with humanity, erasing every trace of sin and sorrow. This consummation fulfills all covenant promises—from Abraham's blessing to Isaiah's new creation prophecies—and roots them in the restored communion between Creator and creature. The river of life and tree of life in the city assure perpetual abundance and healing for the nations (Revelation 22:1–2). Revelation 21:24–26 portrays the nations bringing their glory into the city, symbolizing the complete integration of ethnic diversity into worship. No temple is needed, for "the Lord God the Almighty and the Lamb are its temple" (Revelation 21:22), uniting worship and dwelling in one. This final vision echoes Genesis 1's creation narrative and Psalm 148's universal praise, showing how all creation culminates in Creator–glorification. The eternal state renders war and death obsolete, as God declares, "Behold, I make all things new" (Revelation 21:5). Believers live now with this consummation in view, allowing hope to shape ethics, worship, and mission (Titus 2:13). From triumph on the day of His appearing through millennial reign to final consummation, the story of God's kingdom finds its perfection in the eternal fellowship of the redeemed.

Conclusion

The return of Jesus Christ stands as the great turning point of human destiny: the moment when sorrow will end, every wrong will be righted, and the glory of God will fill both heaven and earth. As we anticipate that day, our call is to live in watchful readiness, to proclaim the gospel without compromise, and to embody the kingdom values of justice, mercy, and love. Whether we face trials or triumphs, we hold fast to the truth that He who promised is faithful, and that when He appears, His appearing will bring fullness of joy to His people and everlasting peace to creation. Maranatha—come, Lord Jesus, come.

Chapter 9. Millennial Reign—A Thousand Years of Peace

The thousand-year reign of Christ offers a vivid portrait of God's restorative purposes unfolding on a cosmic scale. Far beyond earthly utopias or fleeting political triumphs, this era is rooted in divine promise and illustrated by biblical visions—from the binding of evil to the peaceable kingdom where predator and prey coexist in harmony. Scripture beckons us to imagine a world freed from sin's curse, where the King Himself governs with perfect justice, and His people serve as priests and partners in the administration of His righteous rule. In this chapter, we will explore how prophetic Scriptures lay the groundwork for this millennial reality, examine the hallmarks of universal peace and flourishing, and consider the transformative role that resurrected believers will play in stewarding creation. As we reflect on these promises, our hearts are stirred with hope—not for a distant fantasy, but for a divinely ordained future that shapes how we live, work, and worship today.

9.1 Biblical Foundations of the Millennium

9.1.1 Revelation's Binding of Satan

Revelation 20 opens with an angel coming down "from heaven, having the key to the Abyss and a great chain in his hand," seizing the dragon (Satan) and binding him for a thousand years (Revelation 20:1–2). This dramatic action fulfills Isaiah's prophecy that the LORD "will punish Leviathan...the fleeing serpent, Leviathan...the crooked serpent; and he will slay the dragon that is in the sea" (Isaiah 27:1), illustrating divine sovereignty over evil. The binding's purpose—"that he should deceive the nations no more, till the thousand years were finished"—guarantees an era unmarred by demonic deception (Rev 20:3). In this period, the church can experience unprecedented peace, for the principal architect of spiritual warfare is restrained. Early Jewish apocalyptic writings (e.g., 1 Enoch) hint at similar themes, showing that the binding has deep roots in the tradition of final deliverance. The image of a bound serpent also echoes the Eden narrative, where the serpent's head would be crushed (Genesis 3:15), foreshadowing Christ's decisive victory. Moreover, Peter's description of Christ "going and proclaiming to the spirits in prison" (1 Peter 3:19) suggests that prior restraints of evil spirits are part of God's redemptive chronology. The binding underscores that peace in the millennium is not merely human achievement but a gift bestowed once Satan's malign influence is removed. Believers are thus called to anticipate a reign where spiritual warfare gives way to worship and service without hindrance. Finally, the thousand-year timeframe—though debated—serves as a symbolic assurance of complete restoration before the final rebellion and judgment.

9.1.2 Daniel's Prophetic Kingdom

In Daniel 7, the prophet sees four successive beasts representing Babylon, Medo-Persia, Greece, and Rome; then "one like a son of man" approaches the Ancient of Days and is given "dominion and glory and a kingdom, that all peoples, nations, and languages should serve him; his dominion is an everlasting dominion" (Daniel 7:13–14). This vision establishes the pattern: earthly empires rise and fall, but God's kingdom, inaugurated in the person of Christ, endures forever. The "son of man" title emphasizes both divine authority and human solidarity, as Jesus applies it to Himself (Matthew 26:64). Daniel's depiction of successive empires provides historical context, while pointing forward to a transcendent reign that unites all peoples under Messiah's rule. The everlasting nature of this kingdom contrasts with mortal empires, underscoring the permanence of Christ's authority. New Testament writers repeatedly return to Daniel's imagery: Jesus references the Son of Man coming "on the clouds" (Mark 14:62), and Revelation's Lamb–Lion motif echoes Daniel's beasts (Revelation 5:5). The Ancient of Days courtroom scene (Daniel 7:9–10) introduces the judicial aspect of the kingdom, where righteousness will prevail and the "little horn" judged (Daniel 7:26). In the millennial context, Daniel's everlasting dominion begins its earthly phase— mounting to universal peace and justice—before its full consummation in the eternal state. This prophetic cornerstone assures believers that every present difficulty sits within God's sovereign timeline, culminating in the unshakable reign of the Son of Man.

9.1.3 Old Testament Foreshadows

The Old Testament abounds with vivid images prefiguring the millennium. Ezekiel's temple vision (chapters 40–48) portrays a detailed sanctuary with fresh water flowing from its threshold, healing the Dead Sea and yielding abundant fish and fruit for food (Ezekiel 47:1–12). This river of life anticipates the eschatological renewal of creation and the living water Christ offers (John 4:14). Isaiah's prophecy envisions predators and prey dwelling together—"The wolf shall dwell with the lamb...they shall not hurt or destroy in all my holy mountain" (Isaiah 11:6–9)—signifying restored harmony throughout the animal kingdom, emblematic of human peace. Zechariah foretold that "ten men from all the nations...shall take hold of the robe of a Jew, saying, 'Let us go with you, for we have heard that God is with you'" (Zechariah 8:23), indicating Gentile nations streaming to Jerusalem to learn God's ways. These foreshadows collectively depict a transformed world marked by divine presence, communal worship, and ecological restoration. Leviticus 26's blessing and curse section frames obedience to the covenant with promised land fertility and security—principles that find ultimate fulfillment when God's people walk in full covenant faithfulness. In Psalm 72, Solomon's reign foresees a king whose rule extends "from sea to sea" and "the desert...blossoms" (Psalm 72:8, 16), merging geographic and ecological revival with messianic justice. These Old Testament visions, while varied in form—prophetic poetry, apocalyptic temple designs, legal promises—converge on the same theme: God's restorative purposes will culminate in an age of unbroken peace under His sovereign rule. Consequently, the millennium stands as both the fulfillment of ancient hopes and the foundation for New Testament eschatology.

9.2 Characteristics of the Millennium

9.2.1 Universal Peace and Justice

Isaiah's declaration that the nations will "beat their swords into plowshares...neither shall they learn war anymore" (Isaiah 2:4) epitomizes millennial peace, where instruments of death are repurposed for life. This universal cessation of hostilities extends beyond human armies to cosmic powers, for "under his feet" all rivals are subdued (1 Corinthians 15:25). Christ's reign as Prince of Peace (Isaiah 9:6) brings equitable justice: "He will judge the poor...with righteousness" (Psalm 72:2). The millennium thus reverses the curse of Genesis 3, restoring human societies to their intended harmony. Prophets stress that peace will flow from Zion, as God's presence becomes the fountain of righteous governance (Micah 4:2–3). This justice encompasses legal fairness—no corrupt judges— and social equity—no exploitation or oppression—mirroring God's covenantal stipulations (Leviticus 19:15). For the first time, human communities will fully embody the Shalom ethos, where compassion and truth combine (Zechariah 8:16–17). The church today, while living in an age of partial fulfillment, glimpses this peace when persecuted believers "rest from their labors" (Revelation 14:13), foreshadowing the global rest to come. The millennial justice also paves the way for ecological peace—fields lie fallow no more, and every creature finds its rightful place in God's order (Psalm 104:14–23). Ultimately, universal peace and justice in the millennium testify to God's triumphant restoration of creation and covenant.

9.2.2 Physical Restoration of Creation

Romans 8:19–22 describes creation itself "eagerly waits" for the revealing of the sons of God, groaning under the curse. In the millennium, that groaning ceases as the land yields abundant harvests and deserts bloom (Isaiah 35:1–2). The productivity of fields and vineyards returns to Edenic levels, signifying God's blessing on human stewardship (Amos 9:14–15). Waters once lifeless teem with fish, mirroring Ezekiel's river vision and foreshadowing the healing streams of Revelation (Ezekiel 47:9; Revelation 22:1). Climate extremes—droughts, floods, storms—are subdued, as the Creator reins in chaos and reinstates the harmony of the original creation (Job 38:8–11). Wildlife relationships revert to peaceful coexistence, reflecting Isaiah's prophetic tableau of predator and prey at peace (Isaiah 65:25). Humanity participates in this renewal through wise cultivation and conservation, fulfilling the dominion mandate in its intended form (Genesis 1:28). This physical restoration also provides a fitting backdrop for spiritual flourishing: healed bodies, abundant resources, and stable climates foster communities centered on worship and justice. The millennial environment thus stands as both proof of God's power to redeem nature and a reminder that human flourishing is inseparable from ecological health. The restored creation will itself worship the Creator, as "the earth is full of the knowledge of the LORD" (Isaiah 11:9), reinforcing the holistic nature of redemptive renewal.

Ezekiel's millennial temple (Ezekiel 40–48) provides a detailed blueprint: eastward–facing gates, holy chambers, and the glory of the LORD returning to dwell within (Ezekiel 43:1–5). This renewed sanctuary becomes the focal point of worship for "all the tribes of Israel" (Ezekiel 48:1), with daily burnt offerings that sustain fellowship between God and humanity (Ezekiel 46:13–15). Feasts—Passover, Pentecost, Tabernacles—resume their covenant rhythms, drawing pilgrims from every nation to Jerusalem (Zechariah 14:16–19). In this era, the temple's courts are never defiled, for idolatry and uncleanness have been purged (Ezekiel 43:8–9). The perpetual presence of God in the Most Holy Place ensures continuous access to divine instruction and intercession (Psalm 27:4). Levitical musicians and priests serve without interruption, offering praise that echoes through the millennial skies (1 Chronicles 23:5; Psalm 89:1–2). The temple's waters flow from under the threshold, signifying ongoing cleansing and life (Ezekiel 47:1–12). Christ—the true temple (John 2:19–21)—mediates access to the Father, yet the physical temple remains as a tangible witness to Jewish covenantal continuity and global worship. This millennial worship scene underscores that God's ultimate desire is not merely moral renewal but intimate communion with His people in place and ritual, foretaste of the New Jerusalem's eternal fellowship (Revelation 21:22–23).

9.3 Role of the Saints

9.3.1 Reigning with Christ

Revelation 20:4–6 affirms that those "who had been beheaded for the testimony of Jesus…and those who had not worshiped the beast" will live and reign with Christ for a thousand years. Their qualification—faithful witness even unto death (Revelation 2:10)—demonstrates that perseverance under persecution is key to sharing Christ's authority. As co–regents, the saints administer justice, reflecting the biblical paradigm that "judges and officers…shall eat the fruit of their toil" (Isaiah

3:14–15). Paul teaches that believers will judge angels and rule on earth (1 Corinthians 6:2–3), underscoring that millennial reign is not merely symbolic but participatory governance. This reign involves local and regional responsibilities, as saints oversee cities and nations with Christ's wisdom, ensuring laws align with divine righteousness. The inter–generational aspect is clear: the martyrs of past ages join newly redeemed believers in a united council of reigners. Their rulership demonstrates that holiness equips for leadership, for the kingly character of Christ is imparted to His Body (2 Timothy 2:12). Liturgies of glorification—"Worthy is the Lamb" (Revelation 5:12)—anticipate the saints' praise leadership during the millennium. This reign also models servant–leadership, for Christ's example is one of humble service (Mark 10:45). Through reigning with Christ, the saints experience both privilege and responsibility, manifesting God's kingdom values on earth before the final consummation.

9.3.2 Priestly Ministry to the Nations

Exodus 19:6 declares Israel a "kingdom of priests," and in the millennium, this role extends globally: the saints teach divine statutes to every nation (Isaiah 2:3). As priests, believers intercede for the world, maintaining the flow of revelation and mercy from God's throne (Revelation 8:3–4). Their ministry includes sacrificial service—ministering to the needy, caring for refugees, and healing the sick—acts that incarnate God's character (Matthew 25:35–40). The Levitical model of varied offerings—burnt, grain, peace—finds fulfillment in the diverse expressions of worship and service during the millennium. Saints also oversee the ceremonial calendar, ensuring festivals and sabbaths reflect covenant renewal and communal identity. In the role of mediators, they guide national leaders to uphold justice and righteousness (Psalm 72:15). This priestly function demonstrates the church's calling to bridge heaven and earth, interceding for blessing and restraining judgment through faithful prayer. The continual presence of saints in the temple courts (Ezekiel 40:8) underscores that priestly ministry is both heaven–focused and earth–engaged. By serving as priests to the nations, the millennium manifests the universal accessibility of God, as every tongue learns His praise (Philippians 2:11).

9.3.3 Judgment of the Nations

Even in the era of unprecedented peace, the millennial reign includes judicial functions. Jesus' parable of the sheep and goats (Matthew 25:31–46) is echoed as nations continue to be assessed by their treatment of the vulnerable. Saints preside over courts that distinguish righteous service from hypocrisy, ensuring that societal structures remain aligned with covenant ethics. The criteria—feeding the hungry, welcoming strangers, clothing the naked—reinforce that genuine loyalty to the King is measured by compassion (Matthew 25:40). Judges cleanse courts of corruption, recalling Amos's demand that justice roll down like waters (Amos 5:24). Cases involving environmental degradation, economic injustice, or social neglect are heard with divine wisdom, reflecting the righteousness of Christ's judgments (Psalm 96:13). This ongoing administration of justice maintains the integrity of the millennial kingdom, preventing relapse into old patterns of oppression. Liturgical readings from Deuteronomy's cities of refuge (Deuteronomy 19:1–13) find practical application, ensuring fair trial and mercy for unintended offenders. By continuing judgment, the saints affirm that the millennium is not a static idyll but a dynamic enforcement of God's will. This judicial role ultimately prepares the way for the final Great White Throne, where every unrepentant heart receives its eternal sentence (Revelation 20:11–15).

9.4 Nations and Jerusalem

9.4.1 Pilgrimage to the Holy City

During the millennial reign, Jerusalem functions as the world's spiritual capital, drawing pilgrims from every nation to worship the Lord (Zechariah 14:16). Isaiah foretold that "out of Zion shall go forth the law, and the word of the LORD from Jerusalem" (Isaiah 2:3), indicating that divine instruction and justice flow from this center. Each appointed festival—

Passover, Pentecost, Booths—beckons international pilgrims to gather before the millennial temple, reversing the scattering of nations in Babel's aftermath (Leviticus 23; Genesis 11:1–9). These journeys foster intercultural fellowship, as diverse peoples learn Hebrew hymns and covenant statutes side by side (Deuteronomy 31:12–13). The roads to Jerusalem are supernaturally maintained, reminiscent of the way God "made the sea into dry land" for Israel's Exodus (Isaiah 43:16–17), ensuring safe passage during this age of peace. Temporary encampments outside the city allow pilgrims to renew covenant allegiance at the city gates before entering the sanctuary courts (Ezekiel 46:20–24). Even athletes and artisans travel to display their gifts in temple celebrations, symbolizing the integration of art, work, and worship (Exodus 35:30–35). Markets in Jerusalem thrive, but commerce is regulated by equitable laws, preventing exploitation of travelers (Leviticus 25:14). The constant influx of pilgrims sustains Jerusalem's centrality while modeling the global unity of God's people under the Davidic King (Psalm 122:6–9). Thus, pilgrimage in the millennium fulfills ancient prophecies and cements Jerusalem's role as the nexus of divine instruction and communal devotion.

9.4.2 Economic and Cultural Flourishing

In the millennium, global economies prosper under Christ's just governance, exemplified by the vision of "the mountains dripping sweet wine" and "all the hills flow with it" (Joel 3:18). Trade routes radiate out from Jerusalem to international hubs, reminiscent of Tyre's ancient mercantile prominence but freed from greed and injustice (Ezekiel 27:12–25). Merchants exchange goods—spices, textiles, metals—at fair prices established by divine decree, ensuring "just balances, just weights, a just ephah, and a just hin" (Leviticus 19:35–36). Cultural centers of learning emerge in restored cities like Babylon and Nineveh, teaching theology, arts, engineering, and medicine under the guidance of millennial priests (Daniel 2:21). Universities incorporate biblical wisdom into every discipline, reflecting Proverbs' injunction that "the fear of the LORD is the beginning of knowledge" (Proverbs 1:7). Music and the fine arts flourish as reflections of divine creativity—

141

"Sing to the LORD a new song" (Psalm 96:1)—with orchestras performing in temple courts. Architectural marvels blend local styles with temple motifs, signifying unity in diversity. Agricultural innovations—drip irrigation, crop rotation—maximize yields without depleting the land, honoring Genesis' mandate to "tend and keep" creation (Genesis 2:15). Craft guilds uphold ethical standards, viewing work as worship (Colossians 3:23–24). This economic and cultural renaissance demonstrates that peace under Christ's rule transforms every sphere of life, eliminating poverty and ennobling human creativity in service to God.

9.4.3 Tribal Identity and Worship

Ezekiel's final chapters (48) enumerate the allotment of land to the twelve tribes of Israel, each with its own territory and role in sustaining the millennial community. These tribal divisions preserve historical and familial identity while operating under a unified national framework. Festival seasons see tribal delegations bearing offerings at designated gates, showcasing unity in diversity (Ezekiel 45:1–7). Gentile believers, grafted into the olive tree, do not abandon their ethnic cultures but bring their traditions into covenant worship, fulfilling Isaiah's inclusion of foreigners (Isaiah 56:6–7). Scriptural readings rotate through the tribal portions, ensuring every family heritage contributes to the shared narrative of redemption (Nehemiah 8:1–8). Temple musicians include tribal choirs, each singing distinct Psalms drawn from ancestral worship customs (1 Chronicles 25:1–8). Feast processions wind through the tribal allotments, symbolizing the movement of blessing from the center outward (Leviticus 23:39–43). Tribal elders serve as counselors in the courts, providing local, culturally sensitive leadership under Christ's universal rule (Deuteronomy 17:8–13). This tribal organization confirms that unity in Messiah does not erase ethnic particularity but celebrates it, reflecting the multiethnic harmony envisioned in Revelation 7:9–10. Thus, tribal identity and worship in the millennium exemplify a restored Israel enriched by the nations, gathered under the Davidic King.

9.5 Continuity and Discontinuity with the Present Age

9.5.1 Continuity of Nature and Culture

While sin's curse is lifted in the millennium, many aspects of daily life echo our present experience: marriage, family, and community gatherings continue, free from distortion (Matthew 22:30). Couples wed and raise children in safe, nurturing environments, reflecting God's design for covenantal relationships (Ephesians 5:31). Agriculture resumes as a meaningful vocation—plowing, planting, and harvesting provide sustenance and communal solidarity (Psalm 128:1–2). Music, dance, and storytelling flourish as cultural expressions of worship, reminiscent of Psalm 150's call to praise "with tambourine and dance." Craftspeople engage in trades—carpentry, weaving, metallurgy—honoring the skill imparted by "the Spirit of the Lord" (Exodus 31:3–5). Festivals and marketplaces maintain economic vitality, but now all commerce operates under just measurements (Leviticus 19:36), ensuring continuity of crafts and trade. Educational institutions teach both vocational skills and theological truths, blending secular and sacred knowledge (Proverbs 22:6). Hospitality customs thrive, as homes open to pilgrims and strangers alike (Hebrews 13:2). Health and sports competitions reflect human drive for excellence, now expressed in celebration rather than competition for gain (1 Corinthians 9:24). These continuities affirm that the millennium revives human culture in its intended, God-honoring form.

9.5.2 Discontinuity—No Sin, Death, or Decay

Despite these continuities, the millennium is marked by radical discontinuities: sin's root is bound so that no one betrays the King's law (Revelation 20:3). Death, disease, and aging are abolished; "the former things have passed away" (Revelation 21:4), and mortality yields to immortality (1 Corinthians 15:54). Crime, violence, and exploitation become inconceivable, as hearts are fully aligned with God's righteousness (Jeremiah 31:33). Natural disasters, famine, and ecological collapse cease, for "the earth will be full of the knowledge of the LORD" (Isaiah 11:9). Human language no longer fails to convey truth, as deception and slander vanish (Zephaniah 3:13). Skepticism, despair, and fear recede, replaced by unclouded joy in God's presence (Isaiah 35:10). Memory of past evils fades, not in amnesia, but as scars that testify to God's redemptive power (Psalm 103:12). Sinful desires are crucified in us, for the Spirit's indwelling is unimpeded (Galatians 5:16–17). These discontinuities demonstrate that the millennium is not merely an improved era but a foretaste of the new creation's radical renewal.

9.5.3 Role of God's Law and Covenant

Under Christ's reign, God's law is internalized rather than imposed externally: "I will put my Spirit within you, and cause you to walk in my statutes" (Ezekiel 36:27). The Torah's moral imperatives—love, justice, mercy—become the matrix of communal life, guiding decisions from business ethics to family relationships (Micah 6:8). Covenant rhythms—Sabbaths and festivals—continue as commemorations of creation rest (Genesis 2:2–3) and redemption (Deuteronomy 5:15). Unlike our age, where the law convicts and points to Christ, in the millennium the law instructs a willing people, no longer burdened but delighted in divine wisdom (Psalm 1:2). Judges trained in covenant statutes preside in cities of refuge and courts of equity, ensuring societal order reflects God's character (Numbers 35:9–34). This lived covenant fosters social trust: contracts are honored and communities flourish under clear, shared expectations (Proverbs 11:1). Scholars teach the law in temple schools, not as a means of salvation, but as the blueprint for harmonious human flourishing (Matthew 13:52). Thus, the role of God's law in the millennium transitions from tutor to triumphant guide, redounding in hearts renewed by grace (Romans 8:4).

9.6 Transition to the Eternal State

9.6.1 Satan's Final Revolt and Defeat

At the close of the thousand years, Revelation 20:7–9 describes Satan's release and final deception of the nations— a last attempt to overthrow the millennial order. He marshals "Gog and Magog" around the camp of the saints, but "fire came down from heaven and consumed them," instituting decisive judgment (Ezekiel 38:1–23; Revelation 20:9). This revolt demonstrates that even in perfect peace, free will persists until God calls history to its conclusion. The prompt defeat underscores God's unwavering sovereignty: rebellion is crushed instantly, preventing any lasting damage. The Church learns that vigilance and prayer remain vital, for spiritual warfare ends only at the final judgment (Matthew 26:41). This final revolt and defeat serve as a purgative moment, separating all evil before the eternal state. With Satan cast into the lake of fire (Rev 20:10), the fountain of corruption is sealed forever, guaranteeing an irreversible transition to consummation.

9.6.2 Great White Throne and Ultimate Judgment

Following the final revolt, Revelation 20:11–15 unfolds the Great White Throne judgment, where the dead "stood before God, and the books were opened." Every deed—public and private—enters the divine record, and individuals are judged "by what they had done" (Romans 2:6). The Book of Life distinguishes those granted eternal life from those consigned to the second death. This solemn scene affirms that God's justice is meticulous and transparent: no sin escapes notice, and no act of love is forgotten (Revelation 22:12). The fate of the unrepentant—"lake of fire" (Rev 20:14)—underscores the gravity of rejecting God's mercy. Yet for the redeemed, this judgment brings vindication and relief, as every wrong is addressed in God's courtroom. The clarity of judgment reveals God's righteousness to all creation, preparing the way for the new creation's unblemished fellowship. This ultimate judicial act closes the age of preparation and inaugurates the era of consummation. The Church today lives under this promise, balancing reverence and compassion in proclamation, knowing that one day Christ will "bring to light the things now hidden in darkness" (1 Corinthians 4:5).

9.6.3 Emergence of the New Heavens and New Earth

With evil's final eradication, Revelation 21:1–5 describes the birth of the New Heavens and New Earth: "Behold, I make all things new." The New Jerusalem descends, adorned like a bride, uniting God's dwelling with His people (Rev 21:2). Creation's original intent—God walking with humanity in Eden—reaches its fulfillment: "God himself will be with them" (Rev 21:3). The river of life and tree of life appear once more, providing perpetual healing and sustenance (Rev 22:1–2). The curse's remnants—death, sorrow, pain—are gone forever (Rev 21:4), fulfilling Isaiah's "former things will not be remembered" (Isaiah 65:17). The city's gates remain open, symbolizing inseparable access to God and reminding the faithful that "they shall see his face" (Rev 22:4). This eternal state completes the covenant promises: Abraham's blessing to the nations, David's everlasting throne, and the promise of a renewed creation (Genesis 12:3; 2 Samuel 7:16; Isaiah 65:17–25). The New Heavens and New Earth establish the final framework for worship, work, and fellowship, as "the nations will walk by its light" (Rev 21:24). Thus, history's trajectory—from creation and fall through redemption and restoration—culminates in unending communion with the Triune God, fulfilling every divine intention.

Conclusion

The vision of a thousand years of peace proclaims that God's kingdom is both already inaugurated and not yet fully realized. In that season, the scars of history are healed, every nation learns righteousness, and creation itself rejoices under the benevolent reign of the Messiah. Yet these millennial promises are more than eschatological curiosities—they call the church to embody God's justice, mercy, and stewardship in the present age. As we await the dawn of that world-wide Sabbath, we are invited to live as its foretaste: reconciling broken relationships, pursuing environmental renewal, and advancing truth in every sphere. By keeping our eyes fixed on the coming Kingdom, we find the strength to endure hardship, the wisdom to serve faithfully, and the joy of participating in God's grand design for all eternity.

Chapter 10. Great White Throne and Eternal Destinies

The culmination of redemptive history confronts every human soul with the reality of divine judgment and the weight of eternal destiny. As the millennial kingdom closes, the cosmos convenes at the Great White Throne, where the righteous Judge unveils every hidden deed and pronounces final sentences. This moment transcends earthly courts and mortal estimates, revealing God's perfect balance of justice and mercy. Here, the ultimate question is answered—where will each person stand when the curtain of time falls? In this chapter, we explore the significance of the Great White Throne judgment, the criteria by which all are assessed, and the irrevocable destinies that emerge from this solemn tribunal.

10.1 Foundations of Final Judgment

10.1.1 Revelation's Great White Throne

John's vision in Revelation 20:11–12 introduces the Great White Throne: "I saw a great white throne and him who was seated on it. Earth and sky fled from his presence, and no place was found for them." This stark imagery underscores God's unparalleled majesty and the universality of the coming judgment. Every creature—angelic or human—will recognize His authority when creation itself recoils. The "books" opened beside the throne record each person's deeds, linking divine evaluation to tangible moral choices (Rev 20:12). This echoes Daniel's vision that "multitudes who sleep in the dust of the earth...shall awake" and "some to everlasting shame" (Daniel 12:2). The white throne signals purity and justice; no appeal can override the rightful verdict. The scene emphasizes that judgment is not arbitrary but founded on God's transparent record-keeping and righteous standards. John's portrayal warns listeners that hidden sins will become public, urging present repentance. Yet the vision also comforts the faithful, for their righteous acts—however small—are noted and rewarded (2 Tim 4:8). By locating the final judgment in the context of cosmic dissolution ("earth and sky fled"), Revelation affirms that history culminates in God's fair reckoning of every life.

10.1.2 Jesus' Teaching on Final Accountability

Jesus Himself spoke of a coming evaluation when He separates "sheep" from "goats" on the Son of Man's throne (Matthew 25:31–33). He taught that actions toward "the least of these" are in effect service—or rejection—of Him (Matthew 25:40, 45). This parable links final destiny to concrete expressions of mercy and justice, grounding cosmic judgment in everyday ethics. In the Sermon on the Mount, Jesus warned that on that day "not one of your works will remain" unless done in His name (Matthew 7:21–23). He also proclaimed that "everyone will have to give account on the day of judgment for every empty word they have spoken" (Matthew 12:36). His promise that those who endure the gospel's hardships will inherit life (Mark 10:30) contrasts with the condemnation awaiting those who deny Him (Mark 8:38). Jesus framed final judgment as an inevitable encounter—"when the Son of Man comes in his glory" (Matthew 25:31)—urging preparedness and compassion. His teachings make clear that divine justice and mercy converge: kindness done in faith reflects the King's heart, while neglect reveals hardened rebellion. By centering judgment on both faith and works, Jesus upholds Scripture's holistic demands—love of God and neighbor—at the threshold of eternity.

10.1.3 Pauline Perspectives on Judgment

The apostle Paul likewise emphasizes that "we must all appear before the judgment seat of Christ" (Bema) to receive recompense "for what we have done in the body" (2 Corinthians 5:10). He distinguishes this assessment from salvation by grace, noting that believers' works will be tested by fire: "the quality of each person's work will be revealed" (1 Corinthians 3:13). Unburned works commend reward; burned works bring loss but not condemnation, for the worker remains saved "yet so as through fire" (1 Corinthians 3:15). Paul also warns against false confidence, reminding that "God will bring every work into judgment, with every secret thing" (Ecclesiastes 12:14; echoed in Romans 2:16). In Romans 14:10–12, he cites "we will all stand before God's judgment seat," urging mutual humility and responsible stewardship of conscience. His language of rewards—"crowns" for faithfulness, perseverance, and love—reinforces that final judgment includes blessing as well as sentence (1 Thessalonians 2:19; James 1:12). Paul's balanced emphasis on grace and accountability complements Jesus' teaching, portraying judgment as an event of both evaluation and vindication. He assures that those justified by faith will not face condemnation (Romans 8:1), yet calls believers to "work out their salvation with fear and trembling" (Philippians 2:12). Thus, Pauline perspectives reveal final judgment as the culmination of God's restorative work in history and individual lives.

10.2 Criteria and Records

10.2.1 The Books Opened

Revelation 20:12 describes "books" opened alongside the Book of Life, suggesting comprehensive divine record–keeping. These books contain "what had been done," encompassing words, deeds, and possibly hidden motives (Matthew 12:36; Ecclesiastes 12:14). Old Testament antecedents—such as the "Book of the Remembrance of Deeds" in Malachi 3:16 or "books" in Daniel 7:10—establish the motif of God's archives. The transparency of these records means no sin escapes scrutiny, and no righteous act is lost. Jesus warned that "the Son of Man will...repay each person according to what he has done" (Matthew 16:27). The opened books underscore that divine justice is neither capricious nor incomplete but rooted in accurate, unalterable testimony. Believers find assurance that every act of mercy and sacrifice is noted for reward (Hebrews 6:10). The books also eliminate pretense, for deeds done in secret become public, urging integrity in all areas of life. The imagery of multiple volumes suggests that judgment spans moral, relational, and ecological dimensions—every facet of stewardship under God.

10.2.2 The Book of Life

Alongside books of deeds, Revelation 20:12 mentions the Book of Life, which lists those granted eternal life. Individuals whose names appear in this book "will not be thrown into the lake of fire" (Rev 20:15). Old Testament precursors—such as "the book of life of Jerusalem" (Psalm 69:28) and "the book of the living" in Daniel 12:1—affirm that divine election and remembrance guarantee inclusion. Paul echoes this assurance: "Everyone who calls on the name of the Lord will be saved" (Romans 10:13). Yet Revelation 3:5 warns that names may be "blotted out" if not faithful, underscoring perseverance's role. The juxtaposition of two books makes clear that eternal destiny hinges on both grace (Book of Life) and obedience (books of deeds). Intercessory prayers for the nations—"Lord, add them to your number" (Acts 2:47)—reflect hope in their inscription. The Book of Life symbolizes God's covenant loyalty, preserved by Christ's atoning work (Hebrews 12:23). Believers are thus called to "strive to enter" so their names remain permanently in that book (Luke 13:24). The existence of this book reinforces that salvation is not a vague concept but a concrete divine promise recorded in heaven's archives.

10.2.3 The Judge and His Standards

The Great White Throne judgment is overseen by the one "seated on the throne"—the Father in unity with the Son—who renders verdicts with absolute impartiality (Romans 2:11). Jesus taught that the final criteria align with the law's greatest commands: love of God and neighbor (Matthew 22:37–40), demonstrated through acts of mercy (Matthew 25:35–40). Paul clarifies that while righteousness cannot be earned, transformed lives bear fruit compatible with justification (Romans 6:22–23). The judges—themselves saints seated with Christ—serve under His standards, distributing rewards and sentences (1 Corinthians 6:2). Divine standards derive from God's holy character: justice, faithfulness, and love (Psalm 89:14). The inclusion of motivations—"secret things"—indicates that heart attitude matters as much as outward actions (1 Samuel 16:7). This comprehensive standard ensures that both criterion and judge are above reproach, inviting no appeal. The harmonious operation of grace and justice in this judgment reveals God's multifaceted perfections. As finite creatures, we can only glimpse these standards, yet Scripture calls us to align our lives with them now, "knowing that from the Lord you will receive the inheritance as your reward" (Colossians 3:24).

10.3 Eternal Destinies

10.3.1 The Lake of Fire—Second Death

Revelation 20:14–15 defines the lake of fire as the "second death," where death and Hades themselves are cast. This final punishment is reserved for those whose names are not found in the Book of Life and who are judged by their deeds. Jesus warned of this doom: "Depart from me, you cursed, into the eternal fire prepared for the devil and his angels" (Matthew 25:41). The permanence of the lake—no exit or relief—distinguishes it from temporal suffering, affirming the gravity of rejecting God's mercy. Old Testament images of Gehenna portray unquenchable fire as symbolic of divine wrath (Isaiah 66:24). The second death underscores that separation from God is the ultimate tragedy, for "where I am, there you cannot be" (John 13:33). Yet this punishment is neither vindictive cruelty nor accidental; it serves justice and honors the freedom granted to creatures. The reality of the lake of fire motivates evangelism urgency, for many perish for want of hearing the gospel (Romans 10:14–15). Early church fathers affirmed its literal and moral dimensions, cautioning against flippant views of hell. The lake of fire thus solemnly contrasts with the eternal life bestowed on the saved, illustrating the binary outcomes of the Great White Throne.

10.3.2 The New Heavens and New Earth—Eternal Fellowship

Immediately after the judgment, Revelation 21:1–3 unveils the new Heavens and new Earth, where God "will dwell with them, and they shall be his people." This consummation reflects Isaiah's promise of a transformed creation—"I create new heavens and a new earth, and the former things shall not be remembered" (Isaiah 65:17). The New Jerusalem descends as the Bride adorned for her Husband, uniting redeemed humanity with its Creator. No temple is needed, for "the Lord God the Almighty and the Lamb are its temple" (Revelation 21:22), indicating direct, unmediated communion. The river of life and tree of life provide perpetual healing (Revelation 22:1–2), restoring Eden's bounty. Death, mourning, crying, and pain are forever banished (Revelation 21:4), fulfilling God's promise to wipe away every tear. The new creation sustains a community where righteousness dwells, and each person's capacities—rational, relational, aesthetic—find their ultimate expression. This eternal state transcends time, yet flows from the historical work of Christ and the faithful stewarding of creation by His people. The vision of eternity offers present hope, encouraging believers to fix their eyes on "what is unseen" rather than the transient (2 Corinthians 4:18). In the new Heavens and new Earth, God's kingdom reaches its fullest realization, and all who remain in the Lamb's book celebrate unending fellowship.

10.3.3 Implications for Life and Mission

The realities of the lake of fire and the new creation coalesce into a compelling motivation for mission and holy living. Knowing that many stand condemned, the church feels the urgency of Christ's command: "Go therefore and make disciples of all nations" (Matthew 28:19). The promised eternal fellowship galvanizes perseverance through trials, for "our light and momentary affliction...prepares for us an eternal weight of glory" (2 Corinthians 4:17). Ethical decisions— business integrity, environmental stewardship, social justice— gain eternal perspective, as acts done in service to Christ echo in the books opened at the throne (Colossians 3:23–24). Worship takes on renewed reverence, for we stand before the Judge "with our joy full of glory" (Psalm 16:11). The dual hope—avoidance of the second death and entry into the new creation—shapes discipleship, prayer, and community life. Pastors and teachers incorporate these truths to cultivate balanced anxiety and assurance, avoiding both morbid fear and flippant optimism. For individuals, the final destinies affirm the value of every moment: choices today have eternal ramifications. The church's mission thus becomes a foretaste of the new Heavens and new Earth, as believers embody reconciliation, mercy, and truth in anticipation of the eternal state. By embracing both warning and promise, Christians navigate life with holy urgency and steadfast hope.

10.4 Doctrinal and Doxological Implications

10.4.1 The Doctrine of Hell and Righteous Anger

The reality of the lake of fire compels the church to recover a balanced doctrine of hell—one neither trivialized nor sensationalized. Jesus spoke more about Gehenna than Heaven, warning that "it is better for you to enter life crippled than with two hands to go to hell" (Mark 9:43). Paul affirms that God's wrath against ungodliness will be fully expressed in final judgment (Romans 1:18), underscoring that sin bears a cosmic cost. The permanence of the "second death" (Revelation 20:14) reminds us that divine justice respects human freedom: those who persistently reject mercy receive its opposite. Yet righteous anger in Scripture is always God's response to evil and injustice, aimed at correction and vindication (Psalm 7:11; Ephesians 4:26). The church must neither ignore hell nor gloat in it, but preach it as the ultimate demonstration of God's holiness against unrepentant wickedness. Properly held, the doctrine of hell fuels compassion—Jesus wept over Jerusalem (Luke 19:41–44)— and motivates urgent evangelism. It also strengthens pastoral care for those wrestling with sin's consequences, guiding them toward grace (Hebrews 4:15–16). Liturgies that include confessions and prayers for mercy reflect awareness of judgment yet point to the Lamb who takes away sin (John 1:29). In worship, we lift voices in doxologies that celebrate redemption from wrath: "Thanks be to God, who gives us the victory through our Lord Jesus Christ" (1 Corinthians 15:57).

10.4.2 The Doctrine of Heaven and Hope

Just as hell shapes evangelism, the New Heavens and New Earth shape Christian hope. Paul calls God "the God of hope" who fills us with joy and peace as we trust Him (Romans 15:13), a hope anchored not in this world but in the eternal state. Jesus promised His followers a place "so that where I am you may be also" (John 14:3), establishing the doctrine of

Heaven as personal fellowship with Christ. The vision of New Jerusalem descending (Revelation 21:2–3) affirms that Heaven and earth will converge in perfect unity. This hope motivates holiness: "Since everything will be destroyed in this way, what sort of people ought you to be?" (2 Peter 3:11). Hebrews urges us to fix our eyes on Jesus, "who for the joy set before him endured the cross" (Hebrews 12:2), linking future glory to present perseverance. The doctrine of Heaven also informs daily life, as we steward creation in expectation of its renewal (Romans 8:19–22). Liturgical traditions that recite the Apostles' Creed's "I look for the resurrection of the dead and the life of the world to come" embed heavenly hope in worship rhythms. Pastors encourage congregations to meditate on Revelation's imagery—river of life, tree of life (Rev 22:1–2)—so that hope remains vivid amid trial. Thus, the doctrine of Heaven not only consoles but transforms how we live, love, and labor in anticipation of eternity.

10.4.3 Worship in Light of Eternity

Knowing the final destinies transforms our worship: it becomes both doxology for salvation and anticipation of the coming consummation. Revelation's elders fall down before the throne, singing "Worthy is the Lamb" (Rev 5:8–14), modeling eternal worship. Under the Great White Throne's shadow, worship gains urgency—"Sing with joy…it shall be said, 'Give thanks to the LORD, call upon his name'" (Isaiah 12:4). Early Christians met "with glad and sincere hearts" (Acts 2:46), worshiping in homes as a foretaste of communal gathering around Christ's throne. The Eucharist proclaims death until He comes (1 Cor 11:26), linking each celebration to final judgment and hope. Hymns that emphasize His return—"When He shall call me home" or "Soon and very soon"—encourage watchfulness. Corporate prayers often include petitions for Christ's coming—Maranatha—uniting present need with future promise (1 Cor 16:22). When we worship aware of the final reckoning, sermons ground doctrine in eternal realities, avoiding trivializing theology. Artistic expressions—iconography, drama, liturgical dance—draw on eschatological themes to engage senses and affections. Ultimately, worship oriented by eternity shapes character, mission, and community as we live between the now of grace and the not yet of consummation.

10.5 Pastoral and Missional Urgency

10.5.1 Evangelistic Impetus from Judgment

The certainty of final judgment compels the church's missionary zeal: knowing that many stand condemned without Christ (2 Thessalonians 1:8–9), we are sent with urgency. Peter's question—"What good is it if someone gains the whole world and forfeits his soul?" (Mark 8:36)—drives the gospel imperative. Missionary journeys in Acts model this urgency: Paul pressed on "to bear witness to the gospel of the grace of God" despite persecution (Acts 20:24). The knowledge of hell and hope of Heaven must form the backdrop of every evangelistic strategy, ensuring compassion and clarity. Tools like the "sinner's prayer," Gospel dramatizations, or relational evangelism translate eternal truths into accessible contexts. Training programs emphasize cross–cultural sensitivity without compromising the call to repentance (Acts 17:30). Churches mobilize prayer covers—24/7 prayer watches— recognizing spiritual warfare behind lostness (Ephesians 6:18). Short–term mission trips combine proclamation and service, illustrating that urgent souls need both word and deed (Matthew 25:35–40). The Great Commission's "all nations" mandate gains fresh intensity against the backdrop of final destinies (Matthew 28:19–20). Ultimately, awareness of the Great White Throne fuels evangelistic courage, knowing that each life matters infinitely.

10.5.2 Discipleship and Holiness

Judgment teaches that authentic discipleship entails radical obedience—"If anyone seeks to come after me, let him deny himself" (Luke 9:23). Paul's exhortation to "work out your own salvation with fear and trembling" (Philippians 2:12) gains clarity when we recall that every secret thing will be revealed (Ecclesiastes 12:14). Holiness becomes not legalism but grateful response: as recipients of divine mercy, we pursue

Christlikeness (1 Peter 1:15–16). Small groups and accountability partnerships help believers confess sin and spur one another toward love (James 5:16; Hebrews 10:24–25). Spiritual disciplines—fasting, solitude, Scripture meditation—prepare hearts to stand before the throne (Psalm 119:105). Pastoral counseling addresses unresolved guilt by pointing to Christ's atonement, not endless self–condemnation (Romans 8:1). Catechesis in the local church shapes theological literacy, ensuring members know both promises and warnings (Acts 20:27). Church order—including discipline—demonstrates that unrepentant sin risks both relational and eternal consequences (Matthew 18:15–17). The prospect of final accountability refines community life, rooting out hypocrisy and nurturing authenticity. Discipleship thus becomes a journey toward the Day, shaping character and witness in light of the Great White Throne.

10.5.3 Comfort for the Suffering and Bereaved

While the judgment theme can be sobering, it also offers profound comfort to those who suffer in Christ's name. Revelation 6:9–11 depicts martyrs under the altar crying out, "How long…?" until given white robes—symbolizing vindication at the throne. Jesus promised the persecuted that "you will be blessed…for great is your reward in heaven" (Matthew 5:11–12). The certainty that God "will render to each one according to what he has done" (Romans 2:6) reassures believers that suffering is neither wasted nor unnoticed. Pastoral care integrates eschatological hope with present grief: funerals become both farewell and anticipation of resurrection (1 Thessalonians 4:13–18). Hymns like "I'll Fly Away" or "Because He Lives" articulate this comfort. Prayer ministries for the bereaved lean on Scripture: "He will swallow up death forever" (Isaiah 25:8). Ministries to prisoners and persecuted Christians worldwide echo the promise that temporal suffering yields eternal reward (2 Corinthians 4:17). This comfort empowers compassionate outreach—"Weep with those who weep" (Romans 12:15)—as we point suffering souls to the judge who will right all wrongs. Thus, the doctrine of final destinies brings both warning and solace, sustaining the remnant amid trials.

10.6 Living with Eternal Perspective

10.6.1 Prioritizing the Eternal over the Temporal

Paul urges believers to "set your minds on things that are above, not on things that are on earth" (Colossians 3:2), a call sharpened by the reality of final destinies. Investments—time, talents, treasures—gain new meaning when viewed through eternity's lens (Matthew 6:19–21). Acts of service become eternal deposits, as Jesus taught that what we do for "the least of these" we do for Him (Matthew 25:40). Career and leisure choices are reevaluated: will they prepare us for the Great White Throne or merely fill temporal desires? Christian education emphasizes worldview formation, helping students integrate faith with every academic discipline (Romans 12:2). Family devotions recall the promised eternal fellowship, shaping generational faith (Deuteronomy 6:6–7). Mission trips and local outreach projects embody this perspective, as participants encounter the urgency of souls before judgment (1 Corinthians 3:13). Financial stewardship workshops teach giving as preparation for treasury in heaven (Luke 16:9). Regular reflection on Revelation's eschatology prevents complacency and fuels holy ambition. Living with an eternal perspective thus transforms daily choices into steps toward the Great White Throne's Day.

10.6.2 Perseverance in Hope

Hebrews calls us to "run with endurance the race set before us, looking to Jesus" (Hebrews 12:1–2), a metaphor that gains traction when we remember the finish line at final judgment. Trials test our faith but also refine it, as gold is purified by fire (1 Peter 1:7). The martyrs' cry under the altar—"How long?"— is answered by their garments of white, symbolizing patient endurance rewarded at the throne (Revelation 6:11). Paul's declaration—"I have fought the good fight…henceforth there is laid up for me the crown of righteousness" (2 Timothy 4:7–8)—encourages steadfastness. Community support structures—prayer groups, mentoring, pastoral care—sustain believers when discouragement strikes (Galatians 6:2). Daily

Scripture reading keeps hope alive: "Your word is a lamp...a light on my path" (Psalm 119:105). Spiritual songs and hymns recount promise amid pain, reinforcing the conviction that "to me to live is Christ, and to die is gain" (Philippians 1:21). Hope-filled perseverance distinguishes authentic faith, as James affirms that perseverance must finish its work (James 1:4). With eyes fixed on the Great White Throne, believers endure, knowing that faithfulness today yields eternal fellowship.

10.6.3 Anticipation of Resurrection and Restoration

Finally, the certainty of resurrection and new creation sustains hope, for as Jesus declared, "I am the resurrection and the life" (John 11:25). Paul's exultation—"O death, where is your victory?...Thanks be to God, who gives us the victory through our Lord Jesus Christ" (1 Corinthians 15:55–57)—echoes the triumph over sin and death. The promise that "we shall all be changed...in the twinkling of an eye" (1 Corinthians 15:52) motivates holy living in expectancy. Early Christians used the fish symbol as a secret sign of resurrection hope during persecution. Art and architecture in church history depict the empty tomb, reinforcing post–resurrection faith. Modern worship songs like "In Christ Alone" weave resurrection promises into congregational life. Liturgical calendars—Easter, Ascension, Pentecost—celebrate steps toward consummation, anchoring rhythm in eschatological hope. The anticipation of restoration compels environmental stewardship: creation's own liberation awaits (Romans 8:21). Thus, resurrection hope unites present mission with future glory, inviting all who believe to join the song around the throne when the books are opened and new life begins.

Conclusion

The vision of the Great White Throne reminds us that our earthly lives are lived under the gaze of an all-knowing Sovereign whose judgments are just and unerring. While the prospect of final evaluation may stir fear, it also underscores the infinite value of grace extended through Christ—grace that rewrites destinies and secures a place in the Book of Life. As we reflect on the eternal outcomes of that day, we are called to respond with humility, evangelistic urgency, and deeper gratitude for the mercy that precedes judgment. May this sober truth galvanize us to live faithfully, proclaim boldly, and help others prepare for their own meeting with the King.

Chapter 11. New Heavens, New Earth, New Jerusalem

In the consummation of history, God offers a vision of ultimate renewal that surpasses the promise of Eden and fulfills the longing of every heart for true homecoming. The prophetic pages of Scripture culminate in a panorama where heaven and earth converge in perfect harmony, where sorrow, death, and decay are forever banished, and where God Himself dwells openly among His people. This final act of divine creativity restores every facet of creation—cosmic realms, natural landscapes, and human community—into an unbroken symphony of life, beauty, and worship. As we explore this breathtaking vision, we will see how the Scriptures weave together themes of rebirth, covenant fulfillment, and eternal fellowship, calling us to hope beyond present trials and to live in light of the world that is to come.

11.1 Cosmic Renewal

11.1.1 "I Make All Things New"

When God declares, "Behold, I am making all things new," He announces the culmination of His redemptive work and the inauguration of a reality untainted by sin (Revelation 21:5). This echoes Isaiah's promise that He will "create new heavens and a new earth" where former sorrows are forgotten (Isaiah 65:17). The affirmation of continuity and transformation means that what God made in the beginning is honored even as it is gloriously renewed (Genesis 1:1–2; 2 Peter 3:13). The new creation retains its identity but sheds the curse: mountains, seas, and stars endure, now shining with perfected beauty (Psalm 102:25–26). God's creative activity continues, not as a distant act of history, but as a present reality drawing all things toward their intended goal (Colossians 1:16–17). The declaration also implies that every aspect of existence—moral, relational, ecological—falls under God's restorative sovereignty. By making all things new, God validates the goodness of His original design and fulfills His covenant promises to Abraham, David, and the prophets. This cosmic renewal sets the stage for intimate communion: the Creator and His creatures entering into unbroken fellowship. As the "Alpha and Omega," God's finishing work honors His beginning, ensuring that nothing He has made is ultimately wasted (Revelation 22:13). The theme of newness thus permeates the eschatological vision, inviting believers to anticipate and participate in God's ongoing creative renewal.

11.1.2 Dissolution of the Old Order

John's vision describes a dramatic unmaking: "Then I saw a new heaven and a new earth; for the first heaven and the first earth had passed away" (Revelation 21:1). This cosmic dissolution—"earth and sky fled away" (Rev 20:11)—symbolizes the end of sin, death, and decay that once marred creation. Theological significance lies in God's refusal to simply patch over brokenness; He eradicates the old order to establish a wholly righteous reality (2 Peter 3:10–13). The imagery echoes Paul's declaration that the present world is "subject to futility" but awaits liberation into the freedom of the glory of the children of God (Romans 8:20–21). Biblical accounts of flood and fire judgments serve as precursors, showing that divine unmaking always precedes restoration (Genesis 7:11–24; 2 Peter 3:7). Yet the cessation of the old order is neither arbitrary destruction nor eternal oblivion; it is a purposeful clearing away to make room for the fullness of God's life and glory (Isaiah 65:17). The dissolution underscores God's holiness: He cannot abide the persistence of sin's residue. At the same time, it highlights His mercy, for by removing the corrupted structures, He enables perfect fellowship. Ultimately, the dissolution of the old order assures us that no evil endures, and that God's final act is one of holistic renewal rather than mere judgment.

11.1.3 Birth of the New Heavens

The renewed heavens are described as radiant and transparent, reflecting the glory of God and the Lamb as their light (Revelation 21:23). No sun or moon is needed, for God Himself illuminates this realm, signaling the end of natural cycles governed by the curse (Isaiah 60:19–20). The transparency suggests perfect intimacy: no barrier exists between God and His people, as in Eden's unashamed fellowship (Genesis 3:8). The new heavens also function as a canopy of blessing over the new earth, a symbol of God's protective presence (Psalm 104:1–4). Their luminous quality evokes the Shekinah glory that filled the tabernacle and temple (Exodus 40:34–35; 1 Kings 8:11), now extended to all creation. Prophets like Ezekiel anticipated a visible sign of God's return to dwell among His people (Ezekiel 43:2–5), fulfilled in the new heavens' radiance. The birth of the new heavens thus heralds both cosmic and relational renewal: the cosmos itself participates in the worship of its Maker (Psalm 148:1–6). This reborn realm becomes the setting for eternal communion, where human minds and hearts dwell in unbroken awe. Theological reflection on the new heavens invites us to view history not as a static timeline but as a dynamic journey toward divine intimacy. In the birth of the new heavens, believers find assurance that God's ultimate purpose includes both cosmic restoration and personal encounter.

11.2 The New Earth

11.2.1 Restored Landscape

The new earth is portrayed with vivid imagery of vitality: green plains, flowing waters, and crystal seas where life abounds (Revelation 22:1). This restoration echoes Eden's garden, where every tree yielded good fruit and rivers fivefold refreshed the land (Genesis 2:8–14). Isaiah prophesied that deserts would blossom like the rose and that waters would break forth in wilderness regions (Isaiah 35:1–7), testifying to God's power to heal ecological devastation. The absence of thorns and thistles underlines the removal of the curse, permitting unimpeded agriculture and flourishing biodiversity (Isaiah 65:21–23). This geography, "reordered under divine decree," provides both sustenance and beauty, reflecting God's covenantal provision (Psalm 104:10–13). Mountains and valleys are sculpted to facilitate life and beauty, no longer barriers of strife but avenues of blessing (Isaiah 40:4–5). The restored landscape celebrates human stewardship in its intended form: Adam's mandate to "fill the earth and subdue it" realized in harmony with creation (Genesis 1:28). Urban centers integrate seamlessly with nature, as living water flows from temple precincts into public spaces (Ezekiel 47:12). The multiplicity of ecosystems—forests, plains, coasts—sings God's creative diversity, inviting worship from every creature (Psalm 148:7–10). Thus, the new earth's restored landscape embodies the fullness of life and the glory of God's sustaining hand.

11.2.2 Life and Immortality

On the new earth, the foundational promise is "no more death, mourning, crying or pain" (Revelation 21:4), affirming that mortality and suffering are vanquished. Immortal bodies suited to this environment mirror Christ's resurrection body—tangible, yet not subject to decay (1 Corinthians 15:42–44).

The promise of life extends not only to humans but to all creation, groaning in anticipation of redemption (Romans 8:22–23). Prophetic texts envision trees yielding fruit each month, and leaves serving as medicine, symbolizing perpetual vitality and health (Revelation 22:2; Ezekiel 47:12). Communities gather in celebration of life's abundance, free from fear of loss or deprivation (Psalm 16:11). Theological reflection sees this as the fulfillment of typological feasts—Passover's symbol of passing over death, and Tabernacles' water-drawing ceremony—now turned into perpetual reality (Zechariah 14:8–9). Immortality also signifies unbroken fellowship, for death's sting is removed, and the divine presence heals every wound (1 Corinthians 15:54–57). The guarantee of life reshapes ethics: hunger for justice, care for the sick, and compassion for the suffering reflect the life-giving nature of God (Matthew 25:35–40). In this light, eternal life becomes both a gift and a calling—to steward God's life-giving power in community and creation.

11.2.3 Perfected Ecology

Isaiah's portrayal of predator–prey harmony—"the wolf shall dwell with the lamb, and the leopard shall lie down with the young goat" (Isaiah 11:6)—finds literal fulfillment as all creatures live without violence. This ecological perfection underscores God's intent for creation to mirror His character of peace. Rivers teem with fish for food "for the healing of the nations," indicating that ecological health serves both physical and spiritual renewal (Revelation 22:2). Biodiversity flourishes as trees yield fruit monthly, providing both sustenance and aesthetic delight (Revelation 22:2; Psalm 104:14–15). Pollination, seed dispersal, and ecological relationships operate with divine precision, revealing the genius of God's design (Job 12:10). Human communities engage in stewardship without exploitation, honoring the covenantal mandate to "serve and keep" the earth (Genesis 2:15). Seasonal rhythms—spring blossoms, summer harvest, autumn bear—remain but without decay, suggesting a perfected alternation of growth and rest. Creatures extinct or endangered in the present age reemerge, reflecting God's power to resurrect both human souls and ecological networks

(Psalm 104:30). Scientific curiosity is elevated into doxology, as believers study creation's wonders as revelations of the Creator (Psalm 19:1–4). The perfected ecology of the new earth thus embodies holistic redemption, where every ecosystem participates in the praise of God.

11.3 The New Jerusalem

11.3.1 Heavenly City Descends

John's vision of the New Jerusalem descending from heaven "prepared as a bride adorned for her husband" highlights both divine origin and covenant intimacy (Revelation 21:2). Its architecture—high walls, twelve gates named for Israel's tribes, and foundations inscribed with the apostles—symbolizes perfect unity of Old and New Covenants (Revelation 21:12–14). The city's dimensions—twelve thousand stadia—emphasize completeness and divine order (Revelation 21:16). Precious stones and gold reflect light, signifying the glory of God illuminating the city (Revelation 21:18–21). The city's topography—with no temple needed—places God's presence at its heart, uniting worship and habitation (Revelation 21:22). The descent of the city also fulfills prophetic yearnings for Zion's renewal (Isaiah 60:14–15). Its relocation from heaven to earth underscores that human destiny lies in embodied, communal fellowship with God, not disembodied spiritual states. The New Jerusalem is both the culmination of God's redemptive geography and the archetype for redeemed human community. As a bride adorned, it signifies that God rejoices in gifting His people a glorious home. This vision invites believers to gaze beyond the temporary and to orient life around the city yet to come.

11.3.2 Eternal Dwelling of God

Revelation declares, "Behold, the dwelling place of God is with man. He will dwell with them" (Revelation 21:3), fulfilling Eden's original intent for divine–human communion (Genesis 3:8). No temple is needed in the New Jerusalem, for God and the Lamb are its temple, ensuring unmediated access to His presence (Revelation 21:22). This shifts sanctuary theology from a building to the person of Christ and the gathered community. The ceasing of night underscores perpetual revelation: "They need no light of lamp or sun, for the Lord God will be their light" (Revelation 22:5). Immediate fellowship means that prayer, praise, and worship flow continuously, unimpeded by sin or distance. Theological implications include the end of time zones and temporal cycles, as eternity reshapes experience of time and presence. God's throne becomes a communal space, inviting all to approach with confidence and reverence (Hebrews 4:16). The eternal dwelling emphasizes relational over ritual, as the presence of God itself suffices for worship and service. The New Jerusalem thus embodies the climax of covenant intimacy, restoring the fellowship lost in Eden.

11.3.3 Open Gates and Universal Access

The New Jerusalem's gates "will never be shut by day—and there will be no night there" (Revelation 21:25), symbolizing perpetual security and hospitality. Unlike earthly cities that close gates for defense, the heavenly city remains open, reflecting trust in God's protection. Nations bring their glory and honor into the city, affirming that every culture's highest achievements find their place in God's renewed world (Revelation 21:24). The inclusivity of every tribe, tongue, and people echoes the vision of the great multitude in white robes (Revelation 7:9–10). This openness dissolves all barriers— ethnic, social, and geographic—fulfilling Christ's prayer that the church be one as He and the Father are one (John 17:21). The open gates also invite pilgrims from the new earth to enter without hindrance, enabling continuous worship and service. The perpetual access underscores that salvation is offered freely to all who trust the Lamb, without tribal or caste distinctions. As the city's invite extends eternally, so the church's mission extends in time: to call every nation to enter through Christ, the one gate (John 10:9). Thus, the New Jerusalem's open gates embody God's universal hospitality and covenant faithfulness.

11.4 The River and Tree of Life

11.4.1 River of the Water of Life

Revelation 22:1–2 presents a crystal river flowing from the throne of God and of the Lamb, symbolizing the continual outpouring of divine life into creation. This river echoes Ezekiel's vision of waters issuing from the temple, which healed the Dead Sea and brought abundance (Ezekiel 47:1–12). The water's purity—"clear as crystal"—signifies the moral and spiritual cleansing that now characterizes every stream (Proverbs 25:25). Its source at the throne emphasizes that all life and blessing originate in God's sovereign presence (Psalm 36:9). The river's course through the city wards off barrenness, ensuring that the parched places of the new earth are permanently refreshed (Isaiah 41:19). Its healing purpose—"for the healing of the nations"—means that physical and relational wounds are mended, fulfilling Christ's ministry of restoration (Matthew 12:15–17). This provides a vivid contrast to Eden's waters, which merely sustained life; here, they overflow with healing power. Pilgrims drink freely, no longer subject to drought or scarcity (Isaiah 55:1). The river also fosters communion: its banks become meeting places where the redeemed gather to worship and rejoice (Psalm 46:4). In sum, the river of life turns the new city into a perpetual garden, testifying to God's commitment to renew body, soul, and society.

11.4.2 Tree of Life

The Tree of Life stands on both banks of the river, bearing twelve kinds of fruit—one for each month—and its leaves are "for the healing of the nations" (Revelation 22:2). This tree resurrects Eden's original promise (Genesis 2:9), yet now its benefits are limitless and sustained. The twelve fruits symbolize covenantal completeness, uniting Israel's twelve tribes and the church's twelve apostles in a single community of blessing (Revelation 21:12–14). Its monthly yield contrasts with agricultural seasons marked by famine and drought, underscoring the stability of God's supply (Psalm 1:3). The leaves' healing role extends beyond nutrition, providing ongoing restoration for any residual effects of sin or conflict (Isaiah 33:24). Ezekiel foresaw a similar tree that healed the nations (Ezekiel 47:12), linking prophetic hope with apocalyptic fulfillment. The Tree of Life also invites personal intimacy: believers sit under its shade, symbolizing rest and fellowship with God (Isaiah 49:10). Importantly, access to this tree is granted only to the redeemed, illustrating that healing flows through Christ's atoning work (John 6:53–58). Liturgies often reference the Tree of Life to celebrate Christ as the bread of life and the living water (John 4:14; 6:35). Thus, the Tree of Life embodies God's unending provision and the unity of all redeemed peoples in a shared life source.

11.4.3 Access and Prohibition

In the new creation, the curse is lifted—"there shall be no more curse" (Revelation 22:3)—and full access to life's sources is guaranteed for the righteous. Yet Revelation 22:14–15 warns: "Blessed are those who wash their robes...outside are the dogs and sorcerers, and the sexually immoral, and murderers, and idolaters, and everyone who loves and practices falsehood." This juxtaposition highlights that access to eternal blessings requires both cleansing by Christ (Revelation 7:14) and ongoing faithfulness. The prohibition against adding or removing words from the prophecy (Rev 22:18–19) underscores the sacred trust in God's revealed word as the definitive guide to life and destiny. The open invitation—"let the one who is thirsty come; let the one who wishes take" (Rev 22:17)—calls all to faith, yet excludes those who reject the gospel. Access to the river and tree echoes Eden's invitation, but now the guardianship role (Genesis 3:24) is replaced by divine assurance that no guard is needed. The prohibition of unclean influences—"nothing impure will ever enter it" (Revelation 21:27)—ensures that the city remains holy, reflecting God's own character (1 Peter 1:16). The theology of access and exclusion teaches that eternal fellowship is both a gift and a solemn responsibility, rooted in Christ's atoning work and manifested in holy living (Hebrews 12:14). Believers are thus called to both celebrate open doors and respect divine boundaries, living lives that affirm the sacredness of communion in the new creation.

11.5 Eternal Worship and Community

11.5.1 Perpetual Worship before the Throne

Eternal worship is the heartbeat of the new creation: "Day and night they never cease to say, 'Holy, holy, holy, is the LORD God Almighty'" (Revelation 4:8). This unending praise fulfills Isaiah's vision that seraphim surround God's throne, calling His holiness after His cleansing of sin (Isaiah 6:3–7). The continuity of worship underscores its central role: creation exists to glorify its Maker (Psalm 148:1–6). Multilingual choirs—"a great multitude that no one could number" from "every nation, tribe, people and language"—sing salvation's song, embodying Pentecost's promise in everlasting form (Revelation 7:9–10; Acts 2:4). The absence of temple structures (Revelation 21:22) highlights that worship becomes a lived reality, not confined to liturgical settings. The shift from liturgy-bound worship to unmediated adoration mirrors Christ's promise of Spirit-led worship "in spirit and truth" (John 4:23–24). The doxologies of Revelation (5:12; 7:12; 11:17; 19:6) interweave thematic refrains—worth, power, riches—creating an eternal hymn of God's attributes. This perpetual worship sustains the redeemed, for every moment is filled with awareness of God's presence (Psalm 16:11). Thus, worship and community merge into a single, eternal act of adoration, fulfilling creation's original purpose.

11.5.2 The People of God

The New Jerusalem's citizens are named on its gates—twelve tribes of Israel—and its foundations—twelve apostles—symbolizing the unity of God's people across covenants (Revelation 21:12–14). This identity transcends ethnicity: Gentile believers are grafted into Israel's olive tree (Romans 11:17), and Jewish believers find completion in Christ (Romans 11:26). The removal of any barrier—"The wall between Jew and Gentile is broken down" (Ephesians 2:14)—

enables a single, diverse community that honors all backgrounds. Each person bears God's name on their forehead (Revelation 22:4), indicating permanent covenant belonging and divine protection. The image of citizens "serving God" (Revelation 22:3) reverses the fall's alienation: creatures now fulfill their created vocation as worshipers and stewards. The diversity of the people—reflected in languages, cultures, and histories—becomes a testament to God's glory, as every facet of human expression is redeemed. Community life in the city includes mutual care, shared resources, and celebration of differences (Acts 2:44–47). The people's identity is rooted in God as "our God and he will be our guide forever" (Isaiah 52:12). Thus, the new Jerusalem's population exemplifies a reconciled humanity, unified in worship and community.

11.5.3 Servanthood and Priestly Function

As citizens of the new creation, believers "will reign forever and ever" and serve as priests of God and of Christ (Revelation 22:5; 1 Peter 2:9). This dual role merges kingly authority—ruling with Christ (Revelation 5:10)—with priestly mediation—interceding for creation and offering worship. In the millennium, priestly intercession maintained cosmic order; in eternity, that function continues, guiding the nations in worship and wisdom (Revelation 7:15). The concept of servanthood reflects Jesus' model: "The Son of Man came not to be served but to serve" (Mark 10:45), now embodied in the redeemed community's life. Priestly duties include teaching God's ways, administering healing waters, and overseeing festivals that commemorate redemptive history. Unlike Old Testament priests who temporally mediated, the eternal priesthood involves direct fellowship with God—no veil—and ongoing ministry in the light of His presence (Hebrews 10:19–22). Community service extends to creation itself: maintaining the new earth's flourishing and sharing its bounty. The priestly-servant identity ensures that privilege never devolves into hierarchy; every citizen participates in ministry. Thus, servanthood and priesthood in the new creation reflect the gospel's reversal of power structures, centered on humility and divine service.

11.6 Living in the Eternal State

11.6.1 Sustained Communion with God

In the eternal state, the ultimate joy is unbroken fellowship: "They will see his face, and his name will be on their foreheads" (Revelation 22:4). This direct communion fulfills Moses' desire to see God's glory (Exodus 33:18–23) and the promise that "we shall be like him, for we shall see him as he is" (1 John 3:2). The absence of night—"there will be no night there" (Revelation 21:25)—signals perpetual awareness of God's presence, eliminating spiritual darkness. The wearing of God's name signifies covenant belonging and indwelling relationship, transcending any earthly symbol (John 14:23). Eternal communion includes sharing in the divine councils, as Isaiah heard seraphim calling him to service (Isaiah 6:1–8). Prayer becomes immediate and responsive, with no delay or distance between supplicant and Savior. Worship arises naturally from seeing God's beauty unveiled, as "in his presence is fullness of joy" (Psalm 16:11). Communion also involves knowing God intimately—His character, works, and purposes—far beyond our current comprehension (Ephesians 1:17–19). Thus, sustained communion defines eternal existence as relational rather than functional.

11.6.2 Eternal Vocation

The new creation includes meaningful activity: building houses, planting vineyards, and bending swords into plowshares (Isaiah 65:21–22; Micah 4:3). Work, freed from toil and exhaustion, becomes a joyful expression of creativity and service (Psalm 104:23). The arts—music, poetry, visual expression—flourish in worship contexts, reflecting every culture's contribution to praising God (Psalm 150:3–6). Scientific exploration and discovery continue, as creation's depths yield new insights into God's wisdom (Psalm 104:24). Human ingenuity, no longer marred by pride, channels every skill toward stewardship and celebration of the Creator's handiwork. Justice ministries persist—resolving disputes, caring for the vulnerable—ensuring that community life remains just and compassionate (Zechariah 8:19). Education thrives in eternal universities under Christ the Teacher (Matthew 23:8–10), where every discipline integrates divine truth. Hospitality and fellowship flourish, as open gates invite ongoing exchanges among diverse peoples (Revelation 21:25). Thus, the eternal vocation blends worship, work, and wonder in service to God and neighbor, fulfilling humanity's telos.

11.6.3 Hope's Final Consummation

The promise "Surely I am coming soon" (Revelation 22:20) transitions into the eternal refrain as redeemed creation responds, "Amen. Come, Lord Jesus" (Rev 22:20). This final affirmation echoes through the new creation, uniting every voice in the eternal doxology: "To him who sits on the throne and to the Lamb be blessing and honor and glory and might forever and ever!" (Revelation 5:13). The consummation of hope means that every promise—from Abraham's blessing to David's throne—finds fulfillment (Genesis 12:3; 2 Samuel 7:16). Creation itself joins the refrain, as rivers chant God's praises and trees clap their hands (Psalm 98:8–9; Isaiah 55:12). The eternal city, people, and cosmos resonate with the final amen, a collective assent to God's redemptive narrative. This consummation shapes present hope: every act of faith, every note of worship, and every deed of service participates in the green shoot of tomorrow's glory. Living with this final refrain both humbles and exalts believers: humble before God's majesty, exalted in the knowledge that we co–author God's eternal hymn. Thus, hope's final consummation becomes the heartbeat of the new creation, an unending song of redemption's triumph.

Conclusion

The unveiling of the new Heavens, the renewed Earth, and the descending New Jerusalem reminds us that every promise God has spoken will find its yes and amen in the Lord Jesus Christ. This grand finale confirms that nothing in our world is beyond redemption: the skies will shine with uncreated light, the land will teem with life in divine abundance, and humanity will flourish in covenant community around the throne. As we await this glorious reality, our task is to bear faithful witness, to steward creation with foresight, and to cultivate hearts that long for the eternal city. May this vision sustain our hope, shape our worship, and guide our lives until the moment when the King of Glory makes all things new.

Chapter 12. Living the "Come, Lord Jesus" Lifestyle Today

To live in the shadow of Christ's return is to infuse every moment with purpose, passion, and perspective. The "Come, Lord Jesus" lifestyle rejects spiritual complacency, inviting believers to orient their hearts, homes, and habits around the reality that our Savior could appear at any time. This way of life reshapes prayer, worship, community, service, and even suffering—transforming ordinary routines into rehearsals for eternity. As we learn to pray "Maranatha," cultivate disciplines that sharpen our longing, and embody kingdom values in society, we discover that anticipating Christ's advent isn't escapism but the most vibrant, engaged way to live today.

12.1 Cultivating an Eschatological Mindset

12.1.1 Watchfulness and Hope

Jesus repeatedly called His followers to "keep watch" because no one knows the day or hour of His return (Mark 13:33–37; Matthew 24:42). Cultivating watchfulness means living with eyes fixed on eternal realities rather than being lulled by the pleasures or distractions of this world (Colossians 3:1–2). The apostle Peter urges believers to "gird up the loins of your mind, be sober, set your hope fully on the grace to be brought at the revelation of Jesus Christ" (1 Peter 1:13). In practice, that translates into choices—how we spend our time, money, and relationships—being measured against the question, "Will this matter in light of eternity?" (Matthew 6:19–21). Watchfulness also involves spiritual discernment, testing every teaching to ensure it aligns with the Bible's eschatological promises (1 John 4:1–3). Hope, meanwhile, acts as the anchor of the soul in stormy seasons (Hebrews 6:19), fueling perseverance in daily trials (Romans 5:3–5). Early Christians bespoke this balance: during plagues and persecutions they locked doors in prayer, yet remained vigilant for Christ's coming (Acts 12:5–17). Small acts of kindness—feeding the hungry, visiting the prisoner—become expressions of hope, as each kindness points to the King's return to establish justice (Matthew 25:35–40). By combining watchful expectation with active love, believers embody a hope that transforms both their inner lives and their outward witness.

12.1.2 Prayer for Christ's Return

"Maranatha!"—"Come, Lord Jesus"—is both an acclamation and a plea found at the end of 1 Corinthians (16:22). Corporate recitation of this ancient Aramaic cry keeps the church's gaze fixed on the coming Bridegroom. In the Lord's Prayer, we ask "Your kingdom come, Your will be done, on earth as it is in heaven" (Matthew 6:10), weaving eschatological longing into our daily petitions. Fasting and intercession intensify that yearning; Jesus said some spiritual breakthroughs require prayer and fasting (Matthew 17:21), and early church history records periods of citywide fasts before major revivals. A "Maranatha fast" can be observed in Advent seasons or at key moments of communal need, echoing Ezra's call to feasting and fasting for return (Ezra 8:21–23). Personal prayer rhythms—morning, midday, evening—can include explicit petitions for Christ's return: for the ingathering of the nations (Matthew 24:14) and for the church's pure presentation (Ephesians 5:27). Praying with the saints across time links us to the martyrs whose intercession under the altar cried for vindication (Revelation 6:9–11). Integrating eschatological petitions into corporate worship (e.g., "Even so, come, Lord Jesus") creates a shared heartbeat that shapes communal identity and mission. Through persistent, expectant prayer, the church enacts the tension of "already and not yet," affirming God's sovereign timing while pleading for His swift return.

12.1.3 Holiness and Readiness

Anticipating Christ's return compels a lifestyle of holiness: "You also must be ready, for the Son of Man is coming at an hour you do not expect" (Luke 12:40). Scripture calls us to "be holy, for I am holy" (1 Peter 1:15–16), and the vision of the pure New Jerusalem (Revelation 21:27) underscores that nothing impure will enter. Practical disciplines—confession, accountability partners, and regular examination of conscience—help maintain moral alertness (1 John 1:9; James 5:16). Paul exhorts believers to "put to death…earthly members" (Colossians 3:5) and to "put on the Lord Jesus Christ" (Romans 13:14), signaling that readiness requires both denial of sin and proactive pursuit of Christlikeness. Church communities can establish "holiness covenants," small-group commitments to purity and prayer, modeled after Hebrews' call not to "neglect meeting together" (Hebrews 10:25). Seasonal emphases—Lent, Advent—offer annual rhythms for intensified preparation. Scriptural meditations on final accountability ("we must all appear before the judgment seat of Christ" 2 Cor 5:10) fuel sanctified living. Pastors preach not only moral imperatives but the sure hope that Christ "makes us to be a kingdom…having no spot or wrinkle" (Revelation 1:6; Ephesians 5:27). In this way, readiness becomes not burdened legalism but joyous anticipation of our Bridegroom.

12.2 Spiritual Disciplines Oriented Toward the Future

12.2.1 Word-Centered Living

Eschatological discipleship begins and ends with Scripture: meditating on future-focused texts like Daniel 7–12 and Revelation deepens our longing (Psalm 119:15). Lectio divina can be applied to passages such as Revelation 21–22: reading, meditating, praying, and contemplating the text embeds the hope of renewal in our souls. Memorizing key promises—"He who testifies to these things says, 'Surely I am coming soon'" (Revelation 22:20)—sustains perseverance in trials. Small groups dedicate time to study biblical prophecy, avoiding sensationalism by grounding interpretation in sound hermeneutics (2 Timothy 2:15). Teaching future-focused doctrine in Sunday school and Bible studies ensures that eschatology is not marginalized but central to Christian formation. Journaling insights from eschatological readings helps track spiritual growth, linking daily challenges to eternal outcomes. Preaching through Revelation in systematic series shows the unfolding of redemptive history, equipping congregations to live in light of what is to come. Family devotions include reading promises of the new creation, setting children's affections on heavenly realities. By saturating life with God's Word about the end times, believers develop both theological depth and resilient hope.

12.2.2 Prayer and Fasting

Prayer and fasting, practiced by Jesus (Matthew 4:1–2) and the early church (Acts 13:2–3; 14:23), sharpen our spiritual senses and intensify longing for Christ's return. Regular corporate fasts—whether weekly, monthly, or on special days—signal dependence on God and mourning over the world's brokenness (Joel 2:12–13). During fasts, congregations can focus prayer on specific eschatological themes: the purity of the Bride, the advance of the gospel to every nation, and the defeat of evil powers (Revelation 6:9–

11; 14:6–7). Personal fasts, combined with extended prayer times, cultivate humility and create space to hear God's voice regarding our readiness and mission (1 Samuel 1:27–28). Fasting events can incorporate Scripture readings on the kingdom's ethics—justice, mercy, humility—linking physical discipline with moral renewal (Matthew 6:16–18). Historic precedents—Daniel's partial fast (Daniel 10:2–3) and Esther's communal fast (Esther 4:16)—provide models for focused intercession. Through fasting, believers not only deny the flesh but empower their prayers, following Jesus' teaching that some spiritual breakthroughs require it (Mark 9:29). As the body weakens, the spirit strengthens, turning hunger into holy hunger for the Bridegroom's return.

12.2.3 Worship and Communion

The Lord's Supper, celebrated "until He comes" (1 Corinthians 11:26), anchors the church's worship in eschatological hope. Each communion service becomes a rehearsal for the marriage supper of the Lamb (Revelation 19:7–9), reminding participants of Christ's sacrificial love and promised return. Incorporating eschatological hymns—such as "When He Comes" or "Even So, Come"—into corporate worship embeds future-focused truth in congregational song. Liturgy can include responsive readings from Revelation 21–22, inviting the assembly to proclaim the new creation's promises. Visual elements—like banners depicting the New Jerusalem—stimulate imaginations toward eternal realities. Communion devotions may pause for silent reflection on the eschatological significance of the bread and cup, deepening awareness of final fellowship with Christ. Pastors can preach on the "already and not yet," connecting sacramental practice with kingdom anticipation (Luke 22:18). Small-group celebrations of communion on feast days or anniversaries reinforce the sense that each gathering points beyond itself. Thus, worship and communion become daily waysides on the road to eternity, shaping both heart and community.

12.3 Community in Light of the Coming Kingdom

12.3.1 Hope-filled Fellowship

Hebrews exhorts believers to "hold fast...to encourage one another, and all the more as you see the Day approaching" (Hebrews 10:23–25). Hope-filled fellowship begins with sharing stories of God's faithfulness—testimonies that serve as foretaste of triumph over trials (Psalm 66:16). Small groups function as "kingdom cells," where members practice mutual exhortation, pray one another into deeper longing, and study eschatological scripture (Acts 2:42–47). Celebrating baptisms and dedications in the context of kingdom hope reminds new believers that they enter an eternal family. Regular "kingdom nights"—gatherings focused on worship, prophecy, and prayer for revival—reinforce communal expectancy. Seasonal festivals—Pentecost, Advent—can be reclaimed as rehearsals of the ingathering of God's people (Leviticus 23:15–21; Luke 2:25–38). Fellowship meals include discussions of Revelation's visions, integrating hope into everyday table talk. Mentoring relationships between mature saints and new believers emphasize perseverance until the end (2 Timothy 2:2). Thus, fellowship centered on eschatology both strengthens bonds and aligns the community around the "Come, Lord Jesus" hope.

12.3.2 Missional Engagement

Living with the coming kingdom in view transforms mission from program to passion: every outreach project becomes a signpost of the ingathering of the nations (Matthew 24:14). Short-term mission teams articulate that their service in word and deed points to the final restoration of all things (Luke 4:18–19). Contextualization—adapting gospel presentation to local cultures without compromise—reflects Paul's example of becoming "all things to all people" (1 Corinthians 9:22) while keeping Christ at the center. Diaspora ministry—ministering to cross-cultural migrants—models the prophetic promise that foreigners will join themselves to the Lord (Isaiah 56:6). Workplace ministries demonstrate that everyday vocations can advance kingdom values, bearing witness to hope in the public square (Colossians 3:23–24). Digital platforms— podcasts, livestreams, social media—broadcast "Maranatha" prayers and prophecy-driven teachings to a global audience, accelerating the gospel's reach. Partnerships with humanitarian agencies ensure that mercy ministries accompany proclamation, echoing the partnership of Word and Spirit in Acts (Acts 8:5–8). Evaluating any outreach by the question "Does this point people toward Christ's return?" keeps mission rooted in eschatological urgency. Ultimately, missional engagement under the "Come, Lord Jesus" banner calls every believer to be both herald and host of the coming kingdom.

12.3.3 Corporate Worship and Vigil

The early church practiced "all-night" prayer and worship vigils in times of crisis and celebration—such gatherings can be revived on significant eschatological dates (Pentecost, anniversaries of key revivals) to heighten expectancy. Reading Revelation aloud through the night fosters familiarity with prophetic visions, transforming abstract doctrine into vivid experience. Vigil practices—candles, icons of Christ's return, periods of silence—sharpen spiritual sensitivity and remind participants of the coming light that will banish all darkness (John 8:12; Revelation 21:23). Corporate fasting combined with a worship vigil intensifies spiritual warfare prayer, preparing the church to "stand firm against the schemes of the devil" (Ephesians 6:11). Timed readings of Old Testament prophecies—Isaiah 2, Daniel 7, Zechariah 14—interwoven with New Testament visions maintain continuity of divine promise. Testimony times during vigils allow believers to share experiences of God's nearness, prefiguring the unmediated fellowship of the new creation. Intercessory prayer segments focus on the Bridegroom's return, the purity of the Bride, and global evangelization, embodying Revelation's prayers offered before the throne (Revelation 5:8). Vigil worship culminates in a collective "Maranatha" litany, reinforcing communal longing. Through corporate worship and vigil, the church practices living on the edge of eternity, sustained by the promise that He who is faithful will come soon.

12.4 Social Engagement and Justice

12.4.1 Mercy Ministries as Foretaste

Feeding the hungry and clothing the naked (Matthew 25:35–36) become tangible rehearsals of the coming kingdom where every need is met without inequality. Establishing food banks, soup kitchens, and clothing drives echoes Jesus' heart for the poor (Luke 4:18) and points to the banquet feast of the Lamb (Revelation 19:9). Caring for orphans and widows—"religion that is pure and undefiled" (James 1:27)—demonstrates kingdom ethics lived out in community. Health clinics offering free medical care mirror the Tree of Life's leaves "for the healing of the nations" (Revelation 22:2). Refugee resettlement programs enact the welcome of the stranger, foreshadowing the unity of all nations in the New Jerusalem (Revelation 7:9). Advocacy for the incarcerated and their families reflects Jesus' identification with the imprisoned (Matthew 25:36). Holistic ministry teams integrate evangelism with social action, modeling "faith working through love" (Galatians 5:6). Volunteer networks shape neighborhoods as Bermuda triage points for compassion, reducing systemic inequality. Mercy ministries cultivate a prophetic witness, showing that the gospel brings both forgiveness and freedom from oppression. Ultimately, these acts of mercy proclaim that in Christ's kingdom, no one is neglected, and every life is of infinite worth.

12.4.2 Environmental Stewardship

Romans 8:19–21 teaches that all creation awaits liberation from corruption; caring for the environment today is a foretaste of that renewal. Community gardens transform vacant lots into Edenic spaces where neighbors share produce and fellowship, embodying Genesis 2:15's mandate to "work and keep" the land. Recycling, renewable energy initiatives, and water–conservation projects demonstrate responsible dominion under God's sovereignty (Psalm 24:1). Tree-planting campaigns in urban areas echo Joel 2:23's promise of seed-time and harvest, trusting God's blessing on creation. Educational workshops teach creation care as discipleship, showing that environmental ethics flow from love of Creator and neighbor (Matthew 22:39). Church buildings retrofit LED lighting and solar panels, signaling that stewardship of resources honors God (Psalm 50:10–12). Wildlife corridors and native–species restoration programs reflect the prophet's vision of predator–prey harmony (Isaiah 11:6–9). Eco–justice partnerships lobby for policies that protect vulnerable communities from pollution and climate impacts, fulfilling Micah 6:8's call to "do justice." Sabbath observances on environmental scales—land rest, carbon sabbaths—honor God's own rest day model (Exodus 20:8–11). By stewarding God's world, the church anticipates the new earth where creation itself worships its Maker in perfected harmony.

12.4.3 Advocacy and Prophetic Witness

Prophetic witness calls the powerful to account, as Amos declared, "Let justice roll down like waters" (Amos 5:24), reminding society that God's standards transcend human laws. Churches mobilize prayer networks to intercede for legislative reform on issues like human trafficking, mass incarceration, and racial injustice (Proverbs 31:8–9). Public forums and town–hall meetings become platforms where faith voices advocate for the marginalized, reflecting Micah 6:8's call to "act justly." Pastors preach sermons that connect eschatological hope with contemporary ethics, challenging congregations not to wait passively but to "be salt and light" (Matthew 5:13–16). Strategic partnerships with NGOs and community groups foster holistic solutions, blending direct service with systemic change. Social media campaigns highlight injustices, encouraging prayer, donation, and direct action as expressions of kingdom compassion (Isaiah 1:17). Legal aid ministries offer pro bono support, exemplifying Christ's defense of the oppressed (Proverbs 31:9). Educational seminars on ethical consumerism shed light on how purchases either sustain or challenge unjust systems

(James 4:17). Public prayers at civic events testify that ultimate justice belongs to the coming King (Psalm 2:10–12). Through advocacy and prophetic witness, the church signals that the "Come, Lord Jesus" lifestyle involves not only personal piety but also courageous engagement for societal redemption.

12.5 Spiritual Resilience in Suffering

12.5.1 Suffering with Perspective

Viewing trials as "light and momentary affliction" compared to "the eternal weight of glory" (2 Corinthians 4:17) transforms suffering into a means of spiritual growth. When illness, loss, or persecution strike, journaling God's past faithfulness anchors hope in His unchanging character (Psalm 77:11–12). Martyr narratives—such as Stephen's vision of Jesus at the right hand of God (Acts 7:55)—inspire believers to endure with joy, knowing that suffering refines faith (1 Peter 1:6–7). Personal testimonies gathered in small groups create a tapestry of resilience, reminding the community that they are "more than conquerors" (Romans 8:37). Shepherding ministries visit the hospitalized and imprisoned, sharing the gospel's comfort found in Revelation's promise that "God will wipe away every tear" (Revelation 21:4). Counseling programs integrate biblical truth with psychological care, helping individuals process trauma through the lens of redemption (Psalm 34:18). Spiritual retreats focused on lament liturgy—reading Psalms of lament (Psalm 42; 43)—offer safe spaces to bring grief before God. Fasting during times of communal hardship unites congregations in humility and dependence on divine strength (Joel 2:12). Pastors preach messages that frame suffering within God's sovereign plan, fostering courage to face trials (James 1:2–4). By embracing suffering with perspective, the church becomes a crucible of hope, modeling how to live the "Come, Lord Jesus" lifestyle even in darkness.

12.5.2 Encouragement in Trials

Corporate lament and praise in worship services give voice to pain and affirm that God hears our cries (Psalm 42:11). Structured prayer chains pair those in crisis with veteran intercessors, ensuring that no one suffers in isolation (Galatians 6:2). Teaching on the "crown of life" for those who persevere under trial (James 1:12) fosters a disposition of expectation rather than despair. Regular "hope rallies"—gatherings featuring testimonies of deliverance—renew collective courage and trust in God's promises (Psalm 126:2–3). Creative arts therapy classes allow expression of grief and hope through painting, poetry, and music, reflecting Revelation's vision of worship in every form (Revelation 5:8–10). Mentoring relationships between those who have endured serious trials and newer believers foster intergenerational solidarity. Pastoral care teams trained in trauma-informed approaches offer prayerful listening and biblical encouragement. Virtual support groups extend community beyond church walls, enabling global solidarity for persecuted believers (Hebrews 13:3). The church calendar includes "Remembrance Sundays" for collective mourning and proclamation of hope in resurrection (1 Thessalonians 4:13–18). By interweaving lament and promise, the church nurtures resilience, showing that anticipation of Christ's return sustains through even the darkest nights.

12.5.3 Martyrdom and Witness

Studying historic and contemporary martyrs—from Stephen and Polycarp to modern believers in restricted nations—provides models of unwavering faith amid persecution (Hebrews 11:35–40). Educational workshops on the "cost of discipleship" prepare volunteers for potential risks, embedding a realistic understanding of Christian commitment (Matthew 16:24–25). Memorial services for martyrs incorporate Scripture readings (Revelation 6:9–11) and hymns that anticipate their vindication, inspiring gratitude and resolve. Training sessions equip congregants in nonviolent witness and legal rights, enabling them to testify courageously (1 Peter 3:15). Artistic tributes—statues, murals, documentaries—

honor the testimonies of those who "loved not their lives even unto death" (Revelation 12:11). Interfaith dialogues promote religious freedom and highlight the plight of persecuted communities (Acts 16:13–15). Prayer vigils dedicated to regions of high persecution link the local church to the global body, fulfilling Galatians 6:10's call to "do good to all." Literature distribution networks—printing Bibles under the radar—support underground churches, embodying the "even so, come" readiness to share the gospel at cost. By commemorating and learning from martyrs, believers fortify their own witness, recognizing that testimony under trial prefigures the final gathering before the Great White Throne (Revelation 7:9–17). Thus, martyrdom and witness become integral to living the anticipatory lifestyle today.

12.6 Proclaiming the "Come, Lord Jesus" Hope

12.6.1 Bold Evangelism

Integrating the second-coming message into gospel tracts and sermons ensures that every presentation of Christ includes His promised return (Acts 1:11). Street evangelism teams carry banners reading "Maranatha" and distribute invitations to public "Premillennial Bible studies," forming a public testimony. Digital platforms—podcasts, YouTube channels, social media livestreams—spread eschatological teaching to global audiences, fulfilling Romans 10:14–15. Training laypeople in gentle apologetics (1 Peter 3:15) equips them to answer objections to end-times hope and to point skeptics toward the resurrection. Evangelistic conferences feature testimonies from regions where hope sustains believers under persecution (Hebrews 12:1–2). Church outreach events weave live dramatizations of Revelation's visions into gospel presentations, making prophecy accessible. Door-to-door teams carry Bibles and study guides on Revelation 21–22, inviting neighbors to small-group discussions. Campus ministries host "End-Times Café" forums where students debate secular and scriptural worldviews on history's culmination. Partnerships with missionaries in the 10/40 Window ensure that the "everlasting gospel" (Revelation 14:6) reaches unreached peoples. Bold evangelism fueled by eschatological urgency testifies that the gospel is not only about forgiveness but also about the hope of Christ's imminent return.

12.6.2 Cultural Engagement with the Gospel

Artists, musicians, and filmmakers create works that reflect eschatological themes—paintings of the New Jerusalem, songs about resurrection, films on the Rapture—to engage hearts and minds creatively (Philippians 4:8). Corporate worship bands write anthems like "City of Gold" or "Even So, Come," connecting congregations to the coming glory. Literary initiatives encourage novelists and poets to explore redemption themes in speculative fiction, bridging secular and sacred imaginations. Churches host art exhibitions on "Visions of Heaven," drawing community interest and dialogue. Gospel-centered theater productions dramatize Daniel and Revelation narratives, making prophecy tangible. Partnerships with public schools offer after-school arts programs that integrate biblical hope with creative skill development (Matthew 5:16). Podcasts featuring interviews with Christian authors and theologians unpack cultural questions about the end times. Film screenings of unapologetically Christian productions—such as "Left Behind"—are accompanied by panel discussions on biblical prophecy. Visual artists design murals in urban centers depicting scenes of cosmic renewal, sparking curiosity and conversation. Through intentional cultural engagement, the church demonstrates that faith in Christ's return inspires beauty, truth, and hope in all creative endeavors.

12.6.3 Living as Letters to the World

Paul writes, "You are our letter…known and read by all" (2 Corinthians 3:2), calling believers to embody the gospel in visible ways that invite inquiry and reflection. In workplaces, Christians model integrity, kindness, and self–sacrifice, pointing colleagues to the eternal priorities behind their actions (Colossians 3:23–24). Hospitality ministries open homes to neighbors and strangers, reflecting the New Jerusalem's open gates and inclusive fellowship (Revelation 21:25). Everyday acts—paying fair wages, mentoring youth, caring for elderly—demonstrate the "Come, Lord Jesus" ethic of valuing every life (James 2:14–17). Community service projects, from neighborhood cleanups to literacy programs, show that faith without works is dead (James 2:26). Personal testimonies in digital "vlogs" narrate how eschatological hope shapes daily decisions, offering authenticity in a story–hungry culture. Social media posts that highlight Scripture's hope for the new creation go viral, indicating cultural resonance. Christian professionals in medicine, law, and education found ethical committees guided by Revelation's principles, shaping public policy with kingdom values. Artistic tattoos of "Maranatha" become conversation starters, inviting questions about meaning and hope. In all these ways, living letters to the world bear witness that the "Come, Lord Jesus" life is not an otherworldly fantasy but a present reality transforming individuals and societies.

Conclusion

Embracing the "Come, Lord Jesus" lifestyle means walking each day with eyes fixed on the horizon of eternity, allowing that vision to inform our choices, fuel our compassion, and sustain us in trials. It's a call to be spiritually awake, rooted in Scripture, and active in love—bearing witness to the world that our true citizenship lies in a coming Kingdom. As we seek to practice watchfulness, pursue holiness, serve those in need, and proclaim the blessed hope, we become living signposts pointing to the ultimate fulfillment of God's redemptive promise. May our lives echo the church's ancient cry until the day when our longing is finally met: "Even so, come, Lord Jesus."

www.ingramcontent.com/pod-product-compliance
Lightning Source LLC
Chambersburg PA
CBHW060319050426
42449CB00011B/2562

* 9 7 8 1 9 9 7 5 4 1 2 0 2 *